ISBN 978-1-331-59923-4
PIBN 10211056

This book is a reproduction of an important historical work. Forgotten Books uses state-of-the-art technology to digitally reconstruct the work, preserving the original format whilst repairing imperfections present in the aged copy. In rare cases, an imperfection in the original, such as a blemish or missing page, may be replicated in our edition. We do, however, repair the vast majority of imperfections successfully; any imperfections that remain are intentionally left to preserve the state of such historical works.

1 MONTH OF
FREE
READING

at

www.ForgottenBooks.com

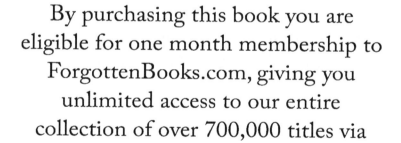

By purchasing this book you are eligible for one month membership to ForgottenBooks.com, giving you unlimited access to our entire collection of over 700,000 titles via our web site and mobile apps.

To claim your free month visit: www.forgottenbooks.com/free211056

English
Français
Deutsche
Italiano
Español
Português

www.forgottenbooks.com

Mythology Photography **Fiction**
Fishing Christianity **Art** Cooking
Essays Buddhism Freemasonry
Medicine **Biology** Music **Ancient
Egypt** Evolution Carpentry Physics
Dance Geology **Mathematics** Fitness
Shakespeare **Folklore** Yoga Marketing
Confidence Immortality Biographies
Poetry **Psychology** Witchcraft
Electronics Chemistry History **Law**
Accounting **Philosophy** Anthropology
Alchemy Drama Quantum Mechanics
Atheism Sexual Health **Ancient History**
Entrepreneurship Languages Sport
Paleontology Needlework Islam
Metaphysics Investment Archaeology
Parenting Statistics Criminology
Motivational

PICTURESQUE

SCOTTISH SCENERY

FROM

ORIGINAL DRAWINGS BY T. L. ROWBOTHAM

MEMBER OF THE SOCIETY OF PAINTERS IN WATER-COLORS

WITH

Archæological, Historical, Poetical, and Descriptive Notes

COMPILED BY

THE REV. W. J. LOFTIE, B.A., F.S.A.

AUTHOR OF "A CENTURY OF BIBLES," "THE LATIN YEAR," ETC., ETC.

New York:

SCRIBNER, WELFORD, & ARMSTRONG, BROADWAY

LONDON: MARCUS WARD & CO.

1875

865
L 82 p

CONTENTS.

CHROMOGRAPHS.

LINLITHGOW.

HE hereditary ill-fortune which pursued all the Scottish kings of the House of Stuart, seems to have doubled its fury when the crown fell to a woman. Mary, Queen of Scotland—or, as she is usually called, Queen of Scots—was unfortunate in all the chief events of her life. Her birth was looked upon as a calamity by her parents and her people; and, as it took place in the old palace of Linlithgow, the name has become closely connected in our minds with hers, and very interesting to all who sympathise in sufferings which, however well they may have been deserved, were undoubtedly of the most severe character, and perhaps quite sufficient to satisfy the sternest judges of her conduct.

It was on Friday, the 8th December, 1542. Her father, who lay upon his death-bed at Falkland, cried out bitterly when he heard the news, and prophesied the extinction of his race. The crown of Scotland came, he said, with a woman into his family, and it would go with one. His words were true so far only as they related to his own immediate branch of the Stuarts. James the

First of England and Sixth of Scotland, who was the son of Mary by her second husband, Henry Stuart, Lord Darnley, carried on the old name, and was the ancestor of three kings and two more queens before the kingdoms they had so persistently misgoverned could bear with their tyranny any longer. The House of Hanover is descended from Queen Mary, but there have been several female links in the line of succession, and the male line of the House of Stuart was itself extinguished at the death of Henry, called the Cardinal of York, in 1808.

Six days after the birth of his daughter, on Thursday, the 14th of December, James the Fifth breathed his last, in disgrace with his subjects for the humiliating defeat of Solway Moss—where he had been beaten by the soldiers of his uncle, Henry VIII. of England— and leaving his kingdom in confusion to be governed by a regent during her long minority. The first six years of the youthful queen's life were passed in Scotland, chiefly at Linlithgow and Stirling; but in 1548 she was sent to the court of France, where she married the Dauphin, afterwards Francis II., and, as his widow, returned to Scotland in 1561; and though very few of the chief events of her troubled reign took place at Linlithgow, she occasionally resided there until her unfortunate marriage with Bothwell, and the flight into England to which it led.

It was in

"Old Linlithgow's crowded town"

that the Regent Murray, the half-brother of Queen Mary, was murdered by Hamilton of Bothwell-haugh in 1570. The story, in its legendary form, has been told by Scott in his wild ballad of "Cadzow Castle," but perhaps the following careful narrative from

the " Life of Mary, Queen of Scots," by M. Mignet, may be accep-
table as an impartial account of the deed. M. Mignet is singularly
free from prejudice in his history, and may be very much depended
on for truthfulness.

"James Hamilton of Bothwell-haugh had sworn a deadly
hatred to the Regent. Taken prisoner at the battle of Langside,
he had recovered his liberty by the arrangement made at Glasgow
on the 13th of March, 1569, by the Regent and the Duke of
Chatelherault. But he had been stripped of all his property.
.   .   .   .   He resolved to slay the Regent, to whom he
attributed the desolation of his household. Several times he attempted to effect his purpose, but without success; his hatred,
encouraged by the Hamiltons, eagerly sought an opportunity for
punishing the author of his ruin, and laying low the oppressor of
his party. This opportunity ere long presented itself.

"The Regent was on his way from Stirling to Edinburgh, and
intended to pass through Linlithgow. In the High Street of this
last-named town, the Archbishop of St. Andrews, uncle of Bothwell-haugh, possessed a house, in front of which Murray and his
cavalcade would necessarily pass. This house was placed at the
disposal of Bothwell-haugh, who made every preparation for the
unfailing performance of the act of vengeance which he had con-
cocted with the Hamiltons. He took his station in a small room
or wooden gallery, which commanded a full view of the street. To
prevent his heavy footsteps being heard, for he was booted and
spurred, he placed a feather-bed on the floor; to secure against any
chance observation of his shadow, which, had the sun broke out,
might have caught the eye, he hung up a black cloth on the oppo-

site wall ; and having barricaded the door in front, he had a swift horse ready saddled in the stable at the back. Even here his preparations did not stop ; for observing that the gate in the wall which enclosed the garden was too low to admit a man on horseback, he removed the lintel-stone, and, returning to his chamber, cut, in the wooden panel immediately below the lattice window where he watched, a hole just sufficient to admit the barrel of his caliver. Having taken these precautions, he loaded the piece with four bullets, and calmly awaited his victim.

" Murray had spent the night in a house in the neighbourhood. Rumours had reached him of the danger by which he was threatened. One of his friends' had even persuaded him to avoid the High Street, and pass round by the back of the town. But the crowd, pressing round him, rendered it impossible for him to do so ; and he rode onwards through Linlithgow, with calm courage, amidst the acclamations of the populace. He proceeded at a slow pace along the High Street till he reached the Archbishop's house. He was thus exposed to the fire of the assassin, who, taking deliberate aim, discharged his caliver. The Regent, shot right through the lower part of his body, fell mortally wounded. At this sight, the crowd rushed towards the house from whence the shot had been fired. But while they were endeavouring to break down the door, Bothwell-haugh, escaping at the back, had mounted his horse, and fled at full speed in the direction of Hamilton Castle."

It is a fact, as the apologists of Mary must regret to remember, that she was so pleased with this atrocious murder that she conferred a pension on the murderer. Hamilton eventually escaped to

France, where he lived for many years. During the contest between the Huguenots and the court party of Catherine de Medici, the mother of Charles IX., Bothwell-haugh was applied to as a desperado ready for any crime, it being hoped he would give his help to a plan for the murder of Coligny; but he considered the proposal an insult. He had slain a man in Scotland, he said, from whom he had suffered a mortal injury; but the world could not tempt him to conspire against one who had in no way harmed him. This story, which Scott repeats, is worthy of notice as a typical example of the strict ideas of honour cherished among people who would hesitate at no crime if personal and revengeful feelings were concerned. Unfortunately for the world, such false ideas of honour are by no means extinct.

The leaders of all parties in Scotland seem to have been relieved by the death of Murray. He had kept a heavy hand upon the lawlessness of the country. The border forays were quickly resumed; while, within the kingdom, successive attempts were made for the supreme power by men whose bloodthirsty violence disgraced every faction alternately. Even the village children, we are told, sided with Mary or her son, and fought as Queen's men or King's men with sticks and stones, and even with more deadly weapons. But we must return to the history of Linlithgow.

In our endeavour to detail the more interesting events of which it was the scene, we have omitted to notice some memorable passages of earlier date. On the site afterwards covered by the palace stood a fort occupied by King Edward the First of England during his invasion of Scotland. It must have been a mere embankment with out-buildings, for we are told that the king, sleeping on the ground and in the open air within the fort, was trodden upon by his horse, and much injured.

James the Fourth of Scotland, who was slain at Flodden by the army of his brother-in-law, Henry the Eighth, resided much at Linlithgow, and added to the building. In *Marmion* (Canto Fourth, XV.–XVII.), Sir Walter Scott thus narrates a legend of this unfortunate king :—

> " Of all the palaces so fair,
>> Built for the royal dwelling,
>> In Scotland, far beyond compare
>> Linlithgow is excelling;
> And in its park, in jovial June,
> How sweet the merry linnet's tune
>> How blithe the blackbird's lay!
> The wild-buck bells from ferny brake,
> The coot dives merry on the lake,
> The saddest heart might pleasure take
>> To see all nature gay.
> But June is to our Sovereign dear
> The heaviest month in all the year:
> Too well his cause of grief you know,—
> June saw his father's overthrow.
> Woe to the traitors, who could bring
> The princely boy against his King!
> Still in his conscience burns the sting.
> In offices as strict as Lent
> King James's June is ever spent.
>
> " When last this ruthful month was come,
> And in Linlithgow's holy dome
>> The King, as wont, was praying;
> While for his royal father's soul
> The chaunters sung, the bells did toll,
>> The Bishop mass was saying—

For now the year brought round again
The day the luckless king was slain—
  In Katharine's aisle the monarch knelt,
  With sackcloth-shirt, and iron belt,
    And eyes with sorrow streaming;
  Around him, in their stalls of state,
  The Thistle's Knight-Companions sate,
    Their banners o'er them beaming.
I too was there, and, sooth to tell,
Bedeafened with the jangling knell,
  Was watching where the sunbeams fell,
    Through the stained casement gleaming;
  But, while I marked what next befel,
    It seemed as I were dreaming.
Stepped from the crowd a ghostly wight,
In azure gown, with cincture white;
His forehead bald, his head was bare,
Down hung at length his yellow hair.—
Now, mock me not, when, good my lord,
I pledge to you my knightly word,
That, when I saw his placid grace,
His simple majesty of face,
His solemn bearing, and his pace
  So stately gliding on,—
Seemed to me ne'er did limner paint
So just an image of the Saint,
Who propped the Virgin in her faint,—
  The loved Apostle John.

" He stepped before the Monarch's chair,
And stood with rustic plainness there,
  And little reverence made ;
Nor head, nor body, bowed nor bent,
But on the desk his arm he leant,
  And words like these he said,

In a low voice,—but never tone
So thrilled through vein, and nerve, and bone :—
   'My mother sent me from afar,
   Sir King, to warn thee not to war,—
    Woe waits on thine array ;
   If war thou wilt, of woman fair,
   Her witching wiles and wanton snare,
   James Stuart, doubly warned, beware :
    God keep thee as He may !'—
The wondering Monarch seemed to seek
   For answer, and found none ;
And when he raised his head to speak,
   The monitor was gone.
The Marshal and myself had cast
To stop him as he outward past ;
But, lighter than the whirlwind blast,
   He vanished from our eyes,
Like sunbeam on the billow cast,
   That glances but, and dies."

After the death of James at Flodden many such stories were commonly reported, as were others that the King had escaped, and would one day return. His son, the father of Queen Mary, succeeded him as James the Fifth at the early age of two years.

The name of Linlithgow is linked with that of another unfortunate monarch. To her is owing much of the picturesque appearance of one of the loveliest ruins in Germany. Elizabeth, Queen of Bohemia, daughter of James the First of England and Sixth of Scotland, passed her early days at this place, and perhaps remembered her Scottish home when the new palace on the banks of the Moselle was planned and built. Many travellers have remarked on the resemblance which undoubtedly exists between the courtyard

of Heidelberg and that of Linlithgow. But much of this similarity
may also be accounted for by the period of their erection, and by
the beauty of the situation of both. The earlier building contains
many marks of a transitional style of architecture, being of that
latest form of Gothic which ran by insensible degrees into the semi-
classical type which we call Elizabethan. Both, too, were eventually destroyed by fire, though Linlithgow survived until 1746,
when it was burnt during the rebellion of the Young Pretender. It
did not, however, owe its destruction to the rebels. After the
battle of Falkirk, the troops of General Hawley, who had been defeated by Prince Charles, retreated first to Linlithgow, which is
only distant some five or six miles from the moor on which the
fight took place ; and having spent the night there, they burnt it
lest it should shelter the pursuing enemy. Sir Walter Scott thus
narrates the circumstances of the battle :—

"The Highland army, lying before Stirling, were regularly
apprized of the movements of the enemy. Upon the 13th of
January, Lord George Murray, who lay at Falkirk, obtained intelligence that the people of the neighbouring town of Linlithgow
had received orders from Edinburgh to prepare provisions and
forage for a body of troops who were instantly to advance in that
direction. Lord George, made aware of Hawley's intention, resolved to move with a sufficient force and disappoint these measures,
by destroying or carrying off the provisions which should be collected in obedience to the requisition.

"The Jacobite general marched to Linlithgow, accordingly,
with the three MacDonald regiments, those of Appin and of Cluny,
and the horse commanded by Elcho and Pitsligo. Parties of the

cavalry were despatched to patrol on the road to Edinburgh for intelligence. About noon, the patrolling party sent back information that they perceived a small body of dragoons, being the advance of General Huske's division, which, as I have stated, marched from Edinburgh that morning. Lord George sent orders to the patrol to drive the dragoons who had shown themselves back upon the main body, if they had one, and not to retire until they saw themselves in danger of being overpowered. In the meantime, he drew up the infantry in line of battle in front of the town of Linlithgow. Lord Elcho, according to his orders, drove back the advanced party of horse upon a detachment of sixty dragoons, and then forced the whole to retire upon a village in which there were masses both of horse and foot. Having thus reconnoitred close up to the main body of the enemy, Lord Elcho sent to acquaint Lord George Murray what force he had in his front, so far as he could discern, and received orders to retreat, leaving a small corps of observation. It was not Lord George's purpose to engage an enemy whose strength, obviously considerable, was unknown to him; he therefore determined to remain in Linlithgow until the enemy arrived very near the town, and then to make his retreat in good order. This object he accomplished accordingly; and, on his repassing the bridge, there was so little distance betwixt the advanced guard of General Huske's division and the rear guard of Lord George Murray's, that abusive language was exchanged between them, though without any actual violence. Lord George continued his retreat to Falkirk, where he halted for that night. On the next day, he again retreated to the villages in the vicinity of Bannockburn, where he learned that General Huske, with half the Government army, had arrived at Falkirk, and that General Hawley had also arrived there on the 16th, with the second division ; that, besides his regular troops, he was joined by 1000 Highlanders, followers of the Argyle family, and that they seemed determined upon battle.

"Upon the 15th and 16th of January, the Chevalier, leaving 1000 or 1200 men under Gordon of Glenbucket, to protect the trenches and continue the blockade of Stirling Castle, drew up his men in a plain about a mile to the east of Bannockburn, expecting an attack.

.   .   .   .

"Hawley at length caught the alarm. He suddenly appeared in front of the camp, and, ordering the whole line to advance, placed himself at the head of three regiments of dragoons, drew his sword, and led them at a rapid pace up the hill called Falkirk moor, trusting by a rapid movement to anticipate the Highlanders, who were pressing on towards the same point from the opposite side of the eminence.

.   .   .   .

"When Hawley set off with his three regiments of dragoons, the infantry of the King's army followed in line of battle, having six battalions in the first line, and the same number in the second. Howard's regiment marched in the rear, and formed a small body of reserve.

"At the moment that the Highlanders were pressing up Falkirk moor on the one side, the dragoons, who had advanced briskly, had gained the eminence, and displayed a line of horse occupying about as much ground as one half of the first line of the Chevalier's army. The Highlanders, however, were in high spirits, and their natural ardour was still farther increased at the sight of the enemy. They kept their ranks, and advanced at a prodigious rate towards the ridge occupied by Hawley's three regiments."

Hawley's men, under his own directions, attacked the rebels. But the cavalry and most of the infantry received a decided check, while three regiments differently commanded were able to hold their ground, and many of the Highlanders fled, imagining the day was lost. Scott sums up the results in the following passage :—

"The advantage, upon the whole, was undeniably with Charles Edward ; but from the want of discipline among the troops he commanded, and the extreme severity of the tempest, it became difficult even to learn the extent of the victory, and impossible to follow it up. The Highlanders were in great disorder. Almost all the second line were mixed and in confusion,—the victorious right had no idea, from the darkness of the weather, what had befallen the left,—nor were there any mounted generals or aides-de-camp, who might have discovered with certainty what was the position of affairs. In the meantime, the English regiments which had been routed fled down the hill in great confusion, both cavalry and infantry, towards the camp and town of Falkirk." Hawley "caused the tents to be set on fire, and withdrew his confused and dismayed followers to Linlithgow, and from thence the next day retreated to Edinburgh, with his forces in a pitiable state of disarray and perturbation. The Glasgow regiment of volunteers fell into the power of the rebels upon this occasion, and were treated with considerable rigour ; for the Highlanders were observed to be uniformly disposed to severity against those voluntary opponents, who, in their opinion, were not, like the regular soldiers, called upon by duty to take part in the contention." Sir Walter thus describes the burning of the ancient palace :— " On the night of the 17th, Hawley's disordered troops were quartered in the palace of Linlithgow, and began to make such great fires on the hearths as to endanger the safety of the edifice. A lady of the Livingstone family, who had apartments there, remonstrated with General Hawley, who treated her fears with contempt. ' I can run away from fire as fast as you can, General,' answered the high-spirited dame, and with this sarcasm took horse for Edinburgh. Very soon after her departure her apprehensions were realised; the palace of Linlithgow caught fire, and was burned to the ground. The ruins alone remain to show its former splendour."

On the whole, then, this is one of the most interesting ruins remaining in Scotland. Its proximity to Edinburgh on the one hand and to Stirling on the other brings it constantly into the narrative of events which took place at one town or the other. Although the town is the capital of a county, it is very small, and does not now contain more than four thousand inhabitants. It is, however, full of curious and picturesque buildings, some of them very ancient, the streets being winding and irregular, and abounding in those features which artists prize most highly. The high roofs, the quaint doorways and windows, the clustered chimneys, harmonise well with the great ruin of the royal palace. There is much to admire in the old tower of the county court-house, although the rest of the building is modern and uninteresting. The church, which was founded by King David the First, has been described as the most important specimen of an ancient parochial edifice now remaining in Scotland, both as to dimensions and also as to architectural features. The chancel alone, which is octagonal in plan, is used now for Divine service; but the whole church consists of a nave with aisles and a transept, and is large, wide, and lofty. The tower formerly supported one of those curious spires which are still to be seen at St. Giles's Cathedral in Edinburgh, at Newcastle-on-Tyne, and at St. Dunstan's in the city of London. The south side of the building is much injured in effect by a debased Gothic addition of the 17th century, which blocks up one of the windows. Mr. Fergusson, in his "History of Architecture," speaks with praise of the windows, and especially notes one as a fine specimen of the Scottish flamboyant style. With regard to the beautiful west doorway, he says that it offers a pleasing example of "the half-continental manner in which that feature was usually treated in Scotland." The window above-mentioned, and several other parts of the church, show strong signs of the foreign influence to which the quaint magnificence of Roslin chapel must be attributed. It was beneath this window, which is in the chapel of St. Catherine, at the extremity of the southern transept, that the apparition already mentioned in a quotation from *Marmion* took place. A piece of stone-carving, which represents the Betrayal and other scenes from the Passion of our Saviour, should be noticed. It formerly, in all probability, stood above the high altar, but is now in the vestry-room.

The remains of the palace are entered from the town by a fine castellated gateway built by King James the Fourth. The church stands near the palace, within the enclosure. The gate is flanked by octagonal towers, and over the central arch are the ensigns of

the four great orders of knighthood to which the king belonged.
For St. George of England—or, as it has been called since the time
of King Edward the Sixth, the Order of the Garter—is the shield
with three lions, which King James's great-grandson was destined to
adopt as part of the arms of his double dignity. Beside them is
the Lion of Scotland, within the double tressure, for the Order of
St. Andrew, which was afterwards revived by his degenerate descendant, James the Second of England and Seventh of Scotland,
in 1687, and finally re-established in its present form by Queen
Anne in 1703. The third shield is that of St. Philip of Castile
and Leon, a Spanish order conferred upon King James by the
father and mother of Queen Catharine of Arragon. The fourth is
that of a French order, and bears the three *fleurs-de-lis*.

There are now no remains of the castle or palace of King David
the First. The fort of which we have spoken in connection with
Edward the First of England was demolished in 1307, and all that
is now to be seen dates since a fire which destroyed the older parts
in 1424. The banqueting hall, which was the largest and most
important apartment, was 94 feet long, and had a high roof supported by wooden beams, the stone brackets from which they
sprung being still visible. A withdrawing-room, called the
Audience Chamber, and the principal guard-room beneath are at
one end of the hall. A fine range of circular-headed windows
lighted the hall in which meetings of the Scottish Parliament—
generally consisting of only one body, where lords and commons
sat together—were often held. The private apartments of the
Royal family were on the opposite side of the quadrangle. Some
of them remain entire, including the bower or boudoir of Queen

Margaret, the neglected wife of James the Fourth. It is situated at the top of a tower staircase, and is commemorated in the lines of Sir Walter Scott (*Marmion*, Canto First, XVII.)—

> " Norham is grim and grated close,
> Hemm'd in by battlement and fosse,
> And many a darksome tower ;
> And better loves my lady bright
> To sit in liberty and light,
> In fair Queen Margaret's bower."

In the fifth canto of the same poem, Sir Walter speaks more distinctly of this chamber. After telling of Lady Heron, and of the Queen of France, at whose instigation the king was said to have undertaken the war against England which ended so disastrously for himself and so many of his bravest subjects, he goes on—

> " And yet the sooth to tell,
> Nor England's fair, nor France's queen,
> Were worth one pearl-drop, bright and sheen,
> From Margaret's eyes that fell ;—
> His own Queen Margaret, who, in Lithgow's bower,
> All lonely sat, and wept the weary hour.
> The Queen sits lone in Lithgow pile,
> And weeps the weary day.
> The war against her native soil,—
> Her monarch's risk in battle broil."

This Queen it was who, being the eldest daughter of Henry the Seventh of England and his wife Elizabeth, the eldest daughter of King Edward the Fourth, became eventually, though not till many years after her own death, the link which united the English and Scottish crowns.

There is not much of interest in the other chambers of Linlith-gow Palace, with one exception. This is the room in which Mary Queen of Scots was born; the rest of the older part of the building consists of a chapel and ante-chapel, and a gallery which runs round the whole of the upper storey. On the north side is an addition made by King James the Sixth when he resided here before his accession to the English throne. A beautiful fountain formerly played in the centre of the court, and much of the fine carving with which it was adorned may still be traced. Linlithgow was famous for its fountains, according to the jingling lines,—

> " Lithgow for wells,
> Glasgow for bells,
> Peebles for clash and lees,
> Falkirk for beans and peas."

The lake flows close up to the palace, the towers being pic-turesquely reflected in its waters. The German poet, Uhland, must have thought of such a scene when he wrote his affecting ballad, "The Castle by the Sea." Such an event as that shadowed forth in his lines may well have taken place here. The opening lines especially suggest Linlithgow, and the view we give would serve well as an illustration of them :—

> " Hast thou seen that castle olden
> That is seated by the sea ?
> How the purple clouds and golden
> Float above it gloriously ?
> How its tones are ever blending
> With the clouds that redly glow ;
> And again are oft descending
> To the waves that roll below."

LOCH LEVEN.

HERE are two Lochs of this name in Scotland. One of them is an inland bay, or what in Norway would be called a "fiord." It is situated in Argyleshire, and is a continuation of Loch Linnhe, the famous Pass of Glencoe being upon its shores. But our present concern is with the lake of this name in Kinross, which has become famous for the Castle, on an islet, in which took place one of the most romantic passages in all the romantic history of Queen Mary. Loch Leven is only a few miles west of the shore of the Firth of Forth, with which it communicates by a little river, running into the sea near the town of Leven. The whole lake is about eleven miles in circumference, and contains several small islands. That one on which the ruins of the ancient castle stand, is about half-a-mile from the western shore, and not far from the town of Kinross, where there is a railway station, and it is thus easily visited from Edinburgh and Glasgow, and is a place of great interest to every Scottish traveller.

The so-called "Castle" only consists of a single tower, now fallen into complete decay, and destitute of architectural interest, though two vaulted chambers still exist to attest its former importance. It may be worth while briefly to detail the story of Queen Mary's imprisonment within its walls ; and, with this view, we may

take our choice of the story as it is in M. Mignet's admirable History, or in the scarcely less veracious pages of Sir Walter Scott's immortal romance, "The Abbot," where the tale is told with those embellishments which he was so well able to supply. To begin with the historian, we read that, in 1567, the marriage of Mary with Bothwell, whom she created Duke of Orkney, gave such offence that a powerful league was formed against her by the nobility, among whom the Earls of Argyll, Athol, and Morton, with Kirkaldy, Laird of Grange, were the most prominent. The Queen fled to Dunbar, and, accompanied by Bothwell, proceeded on the 15th June to Carberry Hill, six miles from Edinburgh, where the confederated lords, with their adherents, met her. After a parley and a short contest, the royal army was disbanded, the Queen and Bothwell being left with only sixty gentlemen and a band of hackbutters. At Mary's request, Bothwell rode away in the direction of Dunbar, having first bidden her farewell, and seen her, as it proved, for the last time. "From this moment," says M. Mignet, "she was a captive in the hands of the confederate lords, who conveyed her at once to Edinburgh." After a few days' delay they determined to commit her to the custody of Lord Lyndsay, Lord Ruthven, and William Douglas of Loch Leven. By virtue of their arrangements, "the unfortunate Queen, during the night of the 16th June, was taken from the palace of her ancestors, mounted on a sorry hackney, and conducted to Loch Leven Castle, by Lyndsay and Ruthven, men of savage manners, even in that age." Scott gives the following description of Loch Leven in "The Abbot":—

"The ancient castle, which occupies an island nearly in the centre of the lake, recalled to the page that of Avenel, in which he

had been nurtured. But the lake was much larger, and adorned
with several islets besides that on which the fortress was situated;
and, instead of being embosomed in hills like that of Avenel, had
upon the southern side only a splendid mountainous screen, being
the descent of one of the Lomond hills, and on the other was surrounded by the extensive and fertile plain of Kinross. Roland
Græme looked with some degree of dismay on the water-girdled
fortress, which then, as now, consisted only of one large Donjon-
keep, surrounded with a court-yard with two round flanking-towers
at the angles, which contained within its circuit some other buildings of inferior importance. A few old trees clustered together,
near the castle, gave some relief to the air of desolate seclusion;
but yet the page, while he gazed upon a building so sequestered,
could not but feel for the situation of a captive Princess doomed to
dwell there, as well as for his own. I must have been born, he
thought, under the star that presides over ladies and lakes of water,
for I cannot by any means escape from the service of the one or
from dwelling in the other. But if they allow me not the fair
freedom of my sport and exercise, they shall find it as hard to
confine a wild-drake as a youth who can swim like one."

The mother of Douglas, who resided at Loch Leven, and
whose hard character fitted her particularly for the post of gaoler,
is thus described in the same work :—

"The station which the Lady of Lochleven now held as the
wife of a man of high rank and interest, and the mother of a lawful
family, did not prevent her nourishing a painful sense of degrada-
tion, even while she was proud of the talents, the power, and the
station of her son, now prime ruler of the State, but still a pledge of

her illicit intercourse. Had James done to her (she said in her secret heart) the justice he owed her, she had seen in her son, as a source of unmixed delight and of unchastened pride, the lawful monarch of Scotland, and one of the ablest who ever swayed the sceptre. The House of Mar, not inferior in antiquity or grandeur to that of Drummond, would then have also boasted a Queen amongst its daughters, and escaped the stain attached to female frailty, even when it had a royal lover for its apology. While such feelings preyed on a bosom naturally proud and severe, they had a corresponding effect on her countenance, where, with the remains of great beauty, were mingled traits indicative of inward discontent and peevish melancholy. It perhaps contributed to increase this habitual temperament, that the Lady Lochleven had adopted uncommonly rigid and severe views of religion, imitating in her ideas of reformed faith the very worst errors of the Catholics, in limiting the benefit of the gospel to those who profess their own speculative tenets."

And Scott's description of the royal prisoner is so graphic that we can hardly omit it here :—

"Her face, her form, have been so deeply impressed upon the imagination, that, even at the distance of nearly three centuries, it is unnecessary to remind the most ignorant and uninformed reader of the striking traits which characterise that remarkable countenance, which seems at once to combine our ideas of the majestic, the pleasing, and the brilliant, leaving us to doubt whether they express most happily the queen, the beauty, or the accomplished woman. Who is there, at the very mention of Mary Stuart's name, that has not her countenance before him, familiar as that of the mistress of his youth, or the favourite daughter of his advanced age? Even those who feel themselves compelled to believe all or much of what her enemies laid to her charge, cannot think without a sigh upon a countenance expressive of anything rather than the foul crimes with which she was charged when living, and which still continue to shade, if not to blacken her memory. That brow, so truly open and regal—those eye-brows, so regularly graceful, which yet were saved from the charge of regular insipidity by the beautiful effect of the hazel eyes which they over-arched, and which seem to utter a thousand histories—the nose, with all its Grecian precision of outline—the mouth, so well proportioned, so sweetly formed, as if designed to speak nothing but what was delightful to hear—the dimpled chin—the stately swanlike neck, form a countenance, the like of which we know not to have existed in any other character moving in that high class of life, where the actresses as well as the actors command general and undivided attention."

Here, then, Mary remained till the 25th July, when a singular scene took place within the castle. Lyndsay and Melville came from Edinburgh bearing the acts which were to deprive her of her sovereignty. Melville saw her first, and explained to her the designs of the victorious lords. He told her that, on her refusal to sign an abdication, they had determined that a public trial was to be substituted for it, and that her defamation would be certain, and the loss of her crown inevitable; whilst, on the other hand, being secretly her friend—at least so he professed himself—he insinuated that any deed signed in captivity, and under fear of her life, would be invalid. Lyndsay next entered, and joined with Melville in persuading the unhappy Queen to sign. Ruthven was soon afterwards introduced, and the scene which followed is thus detailed by Scott:—

"Lord Ruthven had the look and bearing which became a soldier and a statesman, and the martial cast of his form and features procured him the popular epithet of Greysteil, by which he was distinguished by his intimates, after the hero of a metrical romance then generally known. His dress, which was a buff-coat embroidered, had a half-military character, but exhibited nothing of the sordid negligence which distinguished that of Lyndsay. But the son of an ill-fated sire, and the father of a yet more unfortunate family, bore in his look that cast of inauspicious melancholy, by which the physiognomists of that time pretended to distinguish those who were predestined to a violent and unhappy death.

"The terror which the presence of this nobleman impressed on the Queen's mind, arose from the active share he had borne in the slaughter of David Rizzio; his father having presided at the perpetration of that abominable crime, although so weak from long and wasting illness, that he could not endure the weight of his armour, having arisen from a sick-bed to commit a murther in the presence of his Sovereign. On that occasion his son also had attended and taken an active part. It was little to be wondered at that the Queen, considering her condition when such a deed of horror was acted in her presence, should retain an instinctive terror for the principal actors in the murther."

After some conversation, Lord Ruthven "proceeded to read a formal instrument, running in the Queen's name, and setting forth that she had been called at an early age to the administration of the crown and realm of Scotland, and had toiled diligently therein,

until she was in body and spirit so wearied out and disgusted, that
she was unable any longer to endure the travail and pain of State
affairs ; and that since God blessed her with a fair and hopeful son,
she was desirous to ensure to him, even while she yet lived, his succession to the crown, which was his by right of hereditary descent.
'Wherefore,' the instrument proceeded, 'we, of the motherly
affection we bear to our said son, have renounced and demitted,
and by these our letters of free good will renounce and demit, the
Crown, government, and guiding of the realm of Scotland, in favour
of our said son, that he may succeed to us as native Prince thereof,
as much as if we had been removed by decease, and not by our own
proper act.　And, that this demission of our royal authority may
have the more full and solemn effect, and none pretend ignorance,
we give, grant, and commit full and free and plain power to our
trusty cousins, Lord Lyndsay of the Byres, and William Lord
Ruthven, to appear in our name before as many of the nobility,
clergy, and burgesses as may be assembled at Stirling, and there,
in our name and behalf, publicly, and in their presence, to renounce
the Crown, guidance, and government of this our kingdom of
Scotland.' "

The Queen at first absolutely refused her signature to such a
document.　Ruthven behaved with rudeness, and even with violence.
He blamed her for all the misfortunes of Scotland in her time ; he
vowed that the kingdom could no longer endure her rule ; he insisted
on her signature.　She asked a few moments for consideration, and
the lords left her, but returned shortly ; and "when," to continue
the narrative as it is given by Sir Walter, " Lord Ruthven had done
speaking, she looked up, stopped short, and threw down the pen.

'If,' said she, 'I am expected to declare I give away my crown of free will, or otherwise than because I am compelled to renounce it by the threat of worse evils to myself and my subjects, I will not put my name to such an untruth—not to gain full possession of England, France, and Scotland, all once my own, in possession or by right.'

"'Beware, madam,' said Lyndsay, and, snatching hold of the Queen's arm with his own gauntletted hand, he pressed it, in the rudeness of his passion, more closely, perhaps, than he was himself aware of,—'beware how you contend with those who are the stronger, and have the mastery of your fate.

" He held his grasp on her arm, bending his eyes on her with a stern and intimidating look, till both Ruthven and Melville cried shame; and Douglas, who had hitherto remained in a state of apparent apathy, had made a stride from the door, as if to interfere. The rude Baron then quitted his hold, disguising the confusion which he really felt, at having indulged his passion to such extent, under a sullen and contemptuous smile.

" The Queen immediately began, with an expression of pain, to bare the arm which he had grasped, by drawing up the sleeve of her gown, and it appeared that his grasp had left the purple marks of his iron fingers upon her flesh—'My lord,' she said, 'as a knight and gentleman, you might have spared my frail arm so severe a proof that you have the greater strength on your side, and are resolved to use it. But I thank you for it—it is the most decisive token of the terms on which this day's business is to rest. I draw you to witness, both lords and ladies,' she said, shewing the marks of the grasp on her arm, 'that I subscribe these instruments in obedience to the sign-manual of my Lord of Lyndsay, which you may see imprinted on mine arm.'

"Lyndsay would have spoken, but was restrained by his colleague Ruthven, who said to him, 'Peace, my lord. Let the Lady Mary of Scotland ascribe her signature to what she will, it is our business to procure it, and carry it to the Council. Should there be debate hereafter on the manner in which it was adhibited, there will be time enough for it.'

"Lyndsay was silent accordingly, only muttering within his beard, 'I meant not to hurt her; but I think women's flesh be as tender as new-fallen snow.'

"The Queen meanwhile subscribed the rolls of parchment with a hasty indifference, as if they had been matters of slight consequence, or of mere formality. When she had performed this painful task, she arose, and having curtsied to the lords, was about to withdraw to her chamber. Ruthven and Sir Robert Melville made, the first a formal reverence, the second an obeisance in which his desire to acknowledge his sympathy was obviously checked by the fear of appearing in the eyes of his colleagues too partial to his former mistress." Lyndsay knelt and asked her pardon, which she granted him with sweetness and dignity; and so this most singular scene was brought to a close.

We must pass by another strange scene at Loch Leven, when Murray, the captive Queen's half-brother, visited her, and proceed to the climax of the story. George Douglas, the younger son of the stern guardian of the Castle, had become fascinated by the charms of Mary. On the 25th March, after a winter of captivity, lightened only by the hopes of escape and the excitement of secretly communicating with her friends in the outer world, an attempt was made by this infatuated young man to convey her across the lake. She had entered the boat which was to convey her, when one of the boatmen penetrated her disguise, and fearing the severity of the Laird, in spite of her entreaties, and even her commands, took her back to her prison. After this unsuccessful attempt George Douglas was sent away from the castle, but he did not leave the neighbourhood. March and April were passed in vain regrets by the Queen, and in active devotion on the part of Douglas, who at length matured a fresh plan for her delivery. A page—Little Douglas, as he was called—was trusted with the most important part of the design.

"The keys had, with the wonted ceremonial, been presented to the Lady Lochleven. She stood with her back to the casement, which, like that of the Queen's apartment, commanded a view of Kinross, with the church, which stands at some distance from the town, and nearer to the lake, then connected with the town by straggling cottages. With her back to this casement, then, and her face to the table, on which the keys lay for an instant while she tasted the various dishes which were placed there, stood the Lady of Lochleven, more provokingly intent than usual—so at least it seemed to her prisoners—upon the huge and heavy bunch of iron, the implements of their restraint. Just when, having finished her ceremony as taster of the Queen's table, she was about to take up the keys, the page, who stood beside her, and had handed her the dishes in succession, looked side-ways to the churchyard, and exclaimed he saw corpse-candles in the churchyard. The Lady of Lochleven was not without a touch, though a

slight one, of the superstitions of the time; the fate of her sons
made her alive to omens, and a corpse-light, as it was called, in
the family burial-place, boded death. She turned her head towards
the casement—saw a distant glimmering—forgot her charge for
one second, and in that second were lost the whole fruits of her
former vigilance. The page held the forged keys under his cloak,
and with great dexterity exchanged them for the real ones. His
utmost address could not prevent a slight clash as he took up the
latter bunch. 'Who touches the keys?' said the Lady; and while
the page answered that the sleeve of his cloak had stirred them,
she looked round, possessed herself of the bunch which now
occupied the place of the genuine keys, and again turned to gaze
at the supposed corpse-candles.

"'I hold these gleams,' she said, after a moment's consideration,
'to come, not from the churchyard, but from the hut of the old
gardener, Blinkhoolie. I wonder what thrift that churl drives, that
of late he hath ever had light in his house till the night grew deep.
I thought him an industrious, peaceful man.—If he turns resetter of
idle companions and night-walkers, the place must be rid of him.'"

The keys were quickly conveyed to the Queen. The writer
proceeds:—

"'We have but brief time,' said Queen Mary; 'one of the two
lights in the cottage is extinguished—that shows the boat is put
off.'

"'They will row very slow,' said the page, 'or kent where
depth permits, to avoid noise.—To our several gear—I will com-
municate with the good Father.'

"At the dead hour of midnight, when all was silent in the

castle, the page put the key into the lock of the wicket which opened into the garden, and which was at the bottom of a staircase that descended from the Queen's apartment. 'Now, turn smooth and softly, thou good bolt,' said he, 'if ever oil softened rust!' and his precautions had been so effectual, that the bolt revolved with little or no sound of resistance. He ventured not to cross the threshold, but, exchanging a word with the disguised Abbot, asked if the boat were ready?

" 'This half hour,' said the sentinel, 'she lies beneath the wall, too close under the islet to be seen by the warder, but I fear she will hardly escape his notice in putting off again.'

" 'The darkness,' said the page, 'and our profound silence, may take her off unobserved, as she came in. Hildebrand has the watch on the tower—a heavy-headed knave, who holds a can of ale to be the best head-piece upon a night-watch. He sleeps for a wager.'

.   .   .   .

"The ladies were then partly led, partly carried, to the side of the lake, where a boat with six rowers attended them, the men crouched along the bottom to secure them from observation.

.   .   .   .

" 'Pardon me, madam, if I disobey,' said the intractable young man ; and with one hand lifting in Lady Fleming, he begun himself to push off the boat.

"She was two fathoms' length from the shore, and the rowers were getting her head round, when Roland Græme, arriving, bounded from the beach, and attained the boat, overturning Seyton, on whom he lighted. The youth swore a deep but suppressed oath, and stopping Græme as he stepped towards the stern, said, 'Your place is not with high-born dames—keep at the head and trim the vessel.—Now give way—give way.—Row, for God and the Queen!'

"The rowers obeyed, and began to pull vigorously.

. . . .

"The dialogue was here interrupted by a shot or two from one of those small pieces of artillery called falconets, then used in defending castles. The shot was too vague to have any effect, but the broader flash, the deeper sound, the louder return which was made by the midnight echoes of Bennarty, terrified and imposed silence on the liberated prisoners. The boat was alongside of a rude quay or landing-place, running out from a garden of considerable extent, ere any of them again attempted to speak. They landed, and while the Abbot returned thanks aloud to Heaven, which had thus far favoured their enterprise, Douglas enjoyed the best reward of his desperate undertaking, in conducting the Queen to the house of the gardener. Yet, not unmindful of Roland Græme, even in that moment of terror and exhaustion, Mary expressly commanded Seyton to give his assistance to Fleming, while Catherine voluntarily, and without bidding, took the arm of the page. Seyton presently resigned Lady Fleming to the care of the Abbot, alleging he must look after their horses; and his attendants, disencumbering themselves of their boat-cloaks, hastened to assist him.

. . . .

"'Farewell, Father,' said the Queen. 'When we are once more seated at Holyrood, we will neither forget thee nor thine injured garden.'

" 'Forget us both,' said the Ex-Abbot Boniface, 'and may God be with you.'

"As they hurried out of the house, they heard the old man talking and muttering to himself, as he hastily drew bolt and bar behind them.

" 'The revenge of the Douglases will reach the poor old man,' said the Queen. 'God help me, I ruin everyone whom I approach.'

" 'His safety is cared for,' said Seyton; 'he must not remain here, but will be privately conducted to a place of greater security. But I would your Grace were in your saddle.—To horse! to horse!'

The party of Seyton and of Douglas were increased to about ten by those attendants who had remained with the horses. The Queen and her ladies, with all the rest who came from the boat, were instantly mounted; and holding aloof from the village, which was already alarmed by the firing from the castle, with Douglas acting as their guide, they soon reached the open ground, and began to ride as fast as was consistent with keeping together in good order."

M. Mignet thus takes up the narrative:—

"She galloped on till she came to Niddry Castle, Lord Seyton's residence in West Lothian. Here she took a few hours' rest, and then pursued her journey to the strong fortress of Hamilton, where she was received by the Archbishop of St. Andrews, and Lord Claud Hamilton, the latter of whom had met her on the road with fifty horse. On arriving at this place of safety, she issued an appeal to all her partisans. She despatched Heyburn of Riccarton, one of Bothwell's servants, to Dunbar, with the hope that the Castle would be delivered to her, and commanded him to proceed afterwards to Denmark and inform his master that she was again at liberty, and would doubtless soon recover her lost authority."

From the same source we obtain several particulars which do not come out in the novel. Willie Douglas, the page, locked the gate after them as they went out, and threw the keys into the water. In 1805, a boy digging on the sands near Kinross House, when the lake was low during a period of severe drought, found a bunch of keys, five in number, no doubt the very same which figured on this memorable occasion. Other relics were found in 1821, when Loch Leven was partly drained. Among them was a gilt key, possibly a chamberlain's badge of office, bearing the inscription, *Marie Reg. 1565.* The Earl of Morton, who is descended from the elder brother of George Douglas, preserves at his seat, Dalmahoy, near Edinburgh, a folding screen made of tapestry, said to have been worked during her imprisonment by Queen Mary and her maids. It is still unfinished as it was left on her escape. There is evidence in her letters to her former chamberlain, Melville, that she made request for gold and silver thread, silk and needles, suitable for such work.

Miss Strickland has given a minute description of this screen in her " Lives of the Queens of Scotland." She mentions that it is worked in fine tent-stitch, with coloured wools, upon canvas. It is now arranged in three breadths, measuring in all about twelve yards in length, the whole being surmounted by a border. The design was believed by Sir Walter Scott to represent some incidents of a French or Italian romance, but Miss Strickland identified all the scenes with events in the life of Mary herself. We cannot accept this explanation as at all probable. Among the figures one represents a gentleman in a superb dress, who, seated in an arm-chair, bares his leg, and lays it on a block before him, while two executioners prepare to amputate it. Another figure, several times introduced, is standing by ; and this, Miss Strickland thought, was a picture of the angry Queen Elizabeth, upon whose orders the executioners were supposed to wait. It would not be easy to connect this extraordinary scene with anything that occurred in the lives of Mary or of her equally unfortunate husband. Mary was always fond of embroidery, and many pieces besides this have been attributed to her needle, with more or less show of authenticity. Among them are five pieces, also forming a screen, on which the contest of Rehoboam and Jeroboam is depicted ; a history which Queen Mary might well have laid to heart as she worked it on the canvas. But her *chef d'œuvre* seems to have been a Crucifixion, which now belongs to Lord Howard, and which is in one piece, worked in silk. It appears to have been presented by Queen Mary's mother, Mary de Guise, to Mary Fitzalan, daughter of Henry, Earl of Arundel, and afterwards Duchess of Norfolk, ancestress of the present possessor. It bears an inscription on the back which is not easily deciphered, but this seems to be the best explanation.

The escape from Loch Leven was accomplished on the evening of Sunday, the 2nd May, 1568.

DOUNE CASTLE.

OF all the strange characters in Scottish history there is scarcely one more uniformly unpleasant than Margaret Tudor, the daughter of our Henry the Seventh, the sister of our Henry the Eighth, and the wife of James the Fourth, who was slain at Flodden. She seems to have combined in a remarkable degree all the less amiable qualities of her father and her brother. Like the first, she was calculating and cruel, covetous and insincere; like the second, she knew no bounds to the violence of her passions, and was apparently always able to satisfy her conscience as to the justice of any scheme which she wished to gratify. She derived from Edward the Fourth the personal beauty of the Plantagenets, and joining with their haughtiness and their boldness the instability and temper which she inherited from her Welsh ancestors, she became, among the quarrelsome, fierce, uncertain, and revengeful nobles of the northern kingdom, an inciter of quarrels, a leader of the fierce, a by-word for inconstancy, and a cause of feud and bloodshed as long as she lived, and for years after her death. It was her unhappy fate to be at first the wife of a man who was openly unfaithful to her, and to be left under most difficult and trying circumstances without any sincere or disinterested adviser. Her beauty and her misfortunes excite our sympathy, until her errors

and her crimes repel us. She is the most interesting figure in the history of Doune Castle, and for that reason, if for no other, we are obliged to devote a little attention to her life. Much of it was passed at Doune, and the Castle, the greater part of which was probably built by her, or in her time, was by her act, but indirectly, conveyed into the possession of the family by which it is still held after the lapse of three hundred and fifty years.

Doune Castle was built by Murdoch Stewart, second Duke of Albany, nephew of Robert the Third, and Regent of Scotland during the absence in captivity of his cousin King James the First. He was feeble as a ruler, slothful in his own habits, and left to his lawless sons the power of injuring the kingdom by their excesses, and eventually of causing the ruin of their father and his family. King James returned from England in 1424, and, to use the words of Sir Walter Scott—

" The first vengeance of the laws fell upon Murdac, who, with his two sons, was tried and condemned at Stirling for abuse of the King's authority, committed while Murdac was Regent. They were beheaded at the little eminence at Stirling, which is still shown on the Castle Hill. The Regent, from that elevated spot, might have a distant view of the magnificent castle of Doune, which he had built for his residence ; and the sons had ample reason to regret their contempt of their father's authority, and to judge the truth of his words, when he said he would bring in one who would rule them all."

Doune was forfeited to the Crown, and remained part of the Royal estates until 1503, when the marriage of James the Fourth with Margaret Tudor took place, and Doune, with other fair estates, was settled on the bride. Margaret was at this time "an ill-educated girl of fourteen." The king was thirty, and the pair seem to have had from the first little sympathy or affection between them. Miss Strickland says ("Lives of Queens of Scotland," Vol. I., p. 68), "In one taste alone did this dissimilar pair agree, which was in their love for music. The Tudor race had retained their Celtic predilection for that science, and all practically excelled in it. The Royal Stuarts possessed much instrumental skill, together with the inspiration of true poetry. Thus, whatever discrepancies there might have been between James Stuart and Margaret Tudor in age, temper, and talents, they were united in their musical pre-dilections." Their life otherwise seems to have been by no means happy. The Queen had her first son in 1506, but the infant soon died, as did a second; and the boy who was destined to succeed as King James the Fifth was not born until 1512. On the 9th September, 1513, her husband was killed at the fatal battle of Flodden. Margaret became Regent of Scotland, having just completed her twenty-fourth year. In the following April a second son was born to her, the Duke of Ross. But she had not waited for this event before she commenced to look about her for a second husband. In August she was married to Archibald, Earl of Angus, a boy not yet of age. We have no intention of tracing her history during the remainder of the time in which she was united to Angus; it does not concern Doune Castle and its destiny; but in or about 1517 she had changed her views respecting him, and had made up her mind to obtain a divorce, and to find another husband. Her sister-in-law, Katherine of Arragon, who was herself destined to experience the fickleness of the Tudor affections, endeavoured in vain to dissuade her from her purpose. Angus had offended her, and, what was more important, she was in love with another. The handsome Duke of Albany, Regent of Scotland, was the object of her wishes, though he had a wife living at the time. But the divorce was not easily obtained, and several years elapsed before it was pronounced. Meanwhile, two events took place which made a serious difference in her views. She lost her beauty by an attack of small-pox, and she changed her mind about Albany. Towards the end of 1524 she took it into her head to set her affections upon one Henry Stewart, second son of Lord Avondale, the head of a younger branch of the Stewart family. He was lieutenant of her son's body-guard, and she made him Treasurer of Scotland, and, finally, Lord Chancellor. In 1527 the Archbishop of St. Andrews pronounced the divorce, and she lost no time in acting on it. She immediately married Henry Stewart, and after a time he was acknowledged by the King, her son. Miss Strickland writes :— " She had now obtained the end for which she had anxiously striven for more than eight years. Her son had acknowledged her divorce by his recognition and favour to her dear Harry Stuart, who was, from a younger brother and needy courtier, raised to high rank, with the fairest barony in Scotland for his inheritance and that of their children. Her inimical husband, Angus, was soon afterwards chased out of the land into exile in England. Angus had impoverished the Queen by seizing, as her husband, the lands with which she had been richly endowed by the Crown of Scotland on her marriage with James IV. It may be freely inferred that he was forced to yield up his prey, for on his flight to Henry VIII. the young King took possession of his vast property, and divided it amongst those who had aided in the overthrow of the Douglas power. It was not likely that the King forgot to restore his mother to her dower lands. But Henry VIII. treated his sister's divorce from Angus with the utmost contempt, reviled her new spouse, speaking of him disdainfully as 'Lord Muffin,' while he called Angus his dear brother-in-law. Margaret was, however, relieved of the presence of her troublesome spouse for life. She was full of fondness and gratitude to Lord Methven for the assistance he had rendered her son, whom she persuaded to settle on him for life the castellanship of her dower castle of Doune, in the County of Perth. James V. likewise made his new stepfather general of all his artillery, regarding him with constant favour, which he well deserved by his fidelity. Soon after, Lord Methven obtained leave of his sovereign to relinquish Doune Castle in favour of his landless brother, James Stuart, who had served the King faithfully, and even been left for dead at the battle near Linlithgow. James V., with all the generosity of his nature, alienated Doune from the Crown, and settled it on Methven's brother, to the rage and indignation of Queen Margaret, who did not mean to lose the income when she settled it on her new spouse. It was a first quarrel between her and her dear Harry Stuart ; but the offence remained brooding in her mind, until it broke out long years afterwards, according to the malicious nature of the Tudor race."

Thus Doune passed from the Crown to the private family who have held it ever since. Before we detail its subsequent history, it may be interesting to finish that of Queen Margaret. Before many years were past she quarrelled as violently with Henry Stewart, who bore the title of Lord Methven, as ever she had done with

Angus, and but for the special interposition of her son, would have obtained a second divorce. Last of all, she repented of her treatment of Angus; and in 1541 she died, "asking God mercy that she had offended the said Earl as she had." She was buried at Perth with great magnificence, and left, besides her two husbands, several children behind. Her son, James V., was father of Mary, Queen of Scots, and her daughter, Lady Margaret Douglas, was the mother of Henry, Lord Darnley, the husband of that queen.

Doune Castle descended peacefully in the Stewart family. Sir James Stewart obtained custody of it on the 14th July, 1528. Sir James Stewart succeeded him, and a third Sir James married the co-heiress of the Regent Murray—or, as it is now usually spelt, Moray—and with her obtained the earldom which the family still hold.

From this time on, its history is not very eventful. Sir Walter Scott (Notes to *Waverley*) says of it :—

" This noble ruin is dear to my recollection, from associations which have been long and painfully broken. It holds a commanding station on the banks of the River Teith, and has been one of the largest castles in Scotland. Murdock, Duke of Albany, the founder of this stately pile, was beheaded on the Castle-hill of Stirling, from which he might see the towers of Doune, the monument of his fallen greatness.

" In 1745–6, as stated in the text, a garrison on the part of the Chevalier was put into the castle, then less ruinous than at present. It was commanded by Mr. Stewart of Balloch, as governor for Prince Charles; he was a man of property near Callander. This castle became at that time the actual scene of a romantic escape made by John Home, the author of *Douglas*, and some other prisoners, who, having been taken at the battle of Falkirk, were confined there by the insurgents. The poet, who had in his own mind a large stock of that romantic and enthusiastic spirit of adventure which he has described as animating the youthful hero of his drama, devised and undertook the perilous enterprise of escaping from his prison. He inspired his companions with his sentiments, and when every attempt at open force was deemed hopeless, they resolved to twist their bedclothes into ropes, and thus to descend. Four persons, with Home himself, reached the ground in safety. But the rope broke with the fifth, who was a tall, lusty man. The sixth was Thomas Barrow, a brave young Englishman, a particular friend of Home's. Determined to take the risk, even in such unfavourable circumstances, Barrow committed himself to the broken rope, slid down on it as far as it could assist him, and then let himself drop. His friends beneath succeeded in breaking his fall. Nevertheless, he dislocated his ancle, and had several of his ribs broken. His companions, however, were able to bear him off in safety.

"The Highlanders next morning sought for their prisoners with great activity. An old gentleman told the author he remembered seeing the commander, Stewart,

'Bloody with spurring, fiery red with haste,'

riding furiously through the country in quest of the fugitives."

A further description is given in the body of the work. In Chapter XXXVIII. we read of Waverley's visit to Doune after his capture, and on his way to Edinburgh :—

"The country around was at once fertile and romantic. Steep

banks of wood were broken by corn-fields, which this year presented
an abundant harvest, already in a great measure cut down.

" On the opposite bank of the river, and partly surrounded by
a winding of its stream, stood a large and massive castle, the half-
ruined turrets of which were already glittering in the first rays of
the sun. It was in form an oblong square, of size sufficient to contain a large court in the centre. The towers at each angle of the
square rose higher than the walls of the building, and were in their
turn surmounted by turrets, differing in height, and irregular in
shape. Upon one of these a sentinel watched, whose bonnet and
plaid, streaming in the wind, declared him to be a Highlander, as
a broad white ensign, which floated from another tower, announced
that the garrison was held by the insurgent adherents of the House
of Stuart.

" Passing hastily through a small and mean town, where their
appearance excited neither surprise nor curiosity in the few peasants
whom the labours of the harvest began to summon from their re-
pose, the party crossed an ancient and narrow bridge of several
arches, and turning to the left, up an avenue of huge old syca-
mores, Waverley found himself in front of the gloomy yet
picturesque structure which he had admired at a distance. A huge
iron-grated door, which formed the exterior defence of the gateway,
was already thrown back to receive them ; and a second, heavily
constructed of oak, and studded thickly with iron nails, being next
opened, admitted them into the interior court-yard. A gentleman
dressed in the Highland garb, and having a white cockade in his
bonnet, assisted Waverley to dismount from his horse, and with
much courtesy bid him welcome to the castle.

" The governor—for so we must term him—having conducted Waverley to a half-ruinous apartment, where, however, there was a small camp-bed, and having offered him any refreshment which he desired, was then about to leave him.

" ' Will you not add to your civilities,' said Waverley, after having made the usual acknowledgment, ' by having the kindness to inform me where I am, and whether or not I am to consider myself as a prisoner ? '

" ' I am not at liberty to be so explicit upon this subject as I could wish. Briefly, however, you are in the Castle of Doune, in the district of Menteith, and in no danger whatever.'

" ' And how am I assured of that ?'

" ' By the honour of Donald Stewart, governor of the garrison, and lieutenant-colonel in the service of his Royal Highness Prince Charles Edward.' So saying, he hastily left the apartment, as if to avoid further discussion.

" Exhausted by the fatigues of the night, our hero now threw himself upon the bed, and was in a few minutes fast asleep."

LOCH KATRINE.

OCH KATRINE possesses a double interest for the visitor. It is the scene of one of the most charming of romances, and of one of the greatest triumphs of modern engineering skill. This combination is not a very happy one. The sight-seer who only goes to Loch Katrine for the sake of the scenery, and cares for nothing more prosaic than an attempt to identify every situation in the *Lady of the Lake,* must be disappointed in many particulars. He can find nothing which will answer to the Goblin Cave. No tale of real life is connected with the place. The very name which sounds so pretty is in all probability the result of the very bad character the lake once had as the refuge and abode of " caterans," or freebooters. There are several other lakes in Scotland, and even within a short distance of Loch Katrine, which not only equal, but excel it in beauty. Yet such is the subtle charm which Scott has thrown over it, that every turn of the sur-rounding paths, every tree almost, every view, and many things which in another place would be quite destitute of interest, are here invested with a power to touch the imagination and even the heart of thousands. Whatever disappointment we may feel at the place itself is more than compensated by the pleasure to be derived in a fresh reading of Scott's delightful poem. When we have seen the locality it describes, we return with renewed admiration to the

Lady of the Lake, and acknowledging the power of his spell, find more and more cause of amazement at the wonderful genius of the Wizard of the North. The poetry of Scott may not be of the highest kind; it may not abound in flights of sublimity, nor even reach the rugged strength of Burns; but it has one quality which must always—as long, that is, as our language exists—render it a cause of pleasure to all English-speaking and English-reading people—it is true to nature, and it is simple. A child may enjoy *Marmion* or the *Lord of the Isles,* while of the *Lady of the Lake* it is hardly too much to say that it created Loch Katrine.

But to practical people, and also, indeed, to many who love poetry as well, Loch Katrine is the centre of another kind of interest. Near the southern shore a row of shafts rising from the water's edge mark the commencement of the famous aqueduct by which Glasgow, thirty-four miles distant, is supplied with water. Seventy millions of gallons are daily conducted from Loch Katrine by means of piping and tunnelling; and the lake, instead of losing by the withdrawal of such a vast quantity of water, is in reality improved, the level being now, owing to the care taken in penning in the mountain streams, more than five feet higher than before the opening of the works. Loch Katrine is four hundred and fifty feet above the sea, and the fall of the water on its way to Glasgow is thus sufficient for all purposes to which it may be turned. It is difficult not to see in this great and really philanthropical under-taking a matter for reflection, and even for surprise, as great as any which the scenery alone can afford; and before proceeding to describe the lake, under the guidance of the poet, we may pause to look with the engineer at this remarkable and successful triumph of

his art. In a communication to the compiler of Murray's *Hand-
book for Scotland,* Sir George Airy has given an account of the
Glasgow waterworks, from which we venture to quote the following
passages :—

" The singularity which perhaps will first occur to the reader is
that a portion of the waters which, in the course of nature, reached
the sea by the eastern estuary of the Forth, is now turned to the
supply of the great city on the western estuary of the Clyde. This
has arisen from two circumstances. First, that Loch Katrine, the
highest of the reservoirs of water supplying the Forth (by its con-
fluent the Teith), is far west; secondly, that the elevation of Loch
Katrine is considerable. But for the latter circumstance, it would
have been difficult to convey the water of Loch Katrine over the
high ground which divides the basins of the Forth and the Clyde ;
and it was apparently to facilitate this, that the water of Loch
Katrine is now dammed to a height about five feet above its natural
elevation.

. . . .

" Though the Teith, of which Loch Katrine is the head, is an
affluent of the Forth, yet their upper basins, being separated by
hilly ground, must be considered as on different rivers. The basin
of the Forth, whose head is in Ben Lomond, lies between that of
the Teith and that of the Clyde. To gain the basin of the Forth,
it was necessary to pierce the hills bounding the south side of Loch
Katrine. In passing by boat along the lake, from the Trossachs to
the landing-pier of Stronachlachar, the tourist will remark, on the
left hand, a little more than a mile before reaching the pier, the
entrance-works of the water-conduit. They may be visited by a

road from Stronachlachar. They consist of the usual defences against the entrance of extraneous matter, and gates and sluices for regulating the influx of water; well worthy of examination, but requiring no special notice here. The watercourse immediately pierces the hill by a tunnel about a mile long (the air-shafts of which can be seen from the lake), and opens upon one of the streams of Loch Chon, which is a feeder of the Forth. It passes on the south-west sides of Loch Chon and of the upper part of Loch Ard, crosses the Duchray water, passes through a desolate country, crosses many streams of the Forth; and near the summit of the Forth and Clyde Junction Railway, close to the Balfron station, at a height of about two hundred and fifty feet, it quits the basin of the Forth for that of the Endrick, which it subsequently quits at a lower level for that of the Clyde proper.

" The parts, however, which more immediately concern the Loch Katrine tourist are the sluices at the outlets of the lakes. It is obviously necessary to have a sluice at the outlet of Loch Katrine, for maintaining the water at a height sufficient, but not inconvenient, for the discharge into the Glasgow conduit; and this sluice will be found at the bottom of the Beal-nam-bo. It consists, as is usual, of adjustible sliding sluice-gates (managed by rack-and-pinion machinery) and a weir; it also contains, what is less usual, a salmon-ladder, to enable the salmon to leap up into Loch Katrine. This sluice in itself is sufficient for the mere management of the water-supply to Glasgow; but commercial considerations required an additional system of sluices. The streams of the Teith and the Forth are employed to give motion to various mills, and to serve in various manufactures; and, considering the large amount of water abstracted for the supply of Glasgow, there was great fear that in dry seasons the discharge from the outlet of Loch Vennachar would be absolutely stopped, and the mills and manufactures would be deprived of their necessary waters. A large sluice (much larger than that at the outlet of Loch Katrine) is therefore established at the ancient Coilantogle Ford, at the outlet of Loch Vennachar, and is kept under the most careful daily regulation. In wet seasons, the water (which otherwise would have been wasted in an injurious torrent rushing downwards to Stirling and the Forth) is treasured up, raising the surface of Loch Vennachar; and in dry seasons, the water of this accumulated store is discharged, by regulated openings of the sluice-gates, for the benefit of the mills. It was laid down as a condition that the supply of water to the river should never be less than double the minimum in the former state of the lakes, and it is believed that this condition has been maintained without difficulty."

Let us now turn to the less utilitarian aspect of Loch Katrine. Here we cannot do better than follow Sir Walter Scott. With the *Lady of the Lake* in our hands we are under the best guidance. Starting from the little pier at the eastern end, and hardly out of the Trossachs, we find ourselves in a few minutes in the very thick of the romantic associations. The lofty peak of Benvenue towers nearly three thousand feet into mid-air on the left, and forms the best possible background for the view. Thus it is that Scott sees it in the lines (Canto First, xi., xii.) :—

> " The western waves of ebbing day
> Rolled o'er the glen their level way ;

Each purple peak, each flinty spire,
Was bathed in floods of living fire.
But not a setting beam could glow
Within the dark ravines below,
Where twined the path in shadow hid,
Round many a rocky pyramid,
Shooting abruptly from the dell
Its thunder-splintered pinnacle;
Round many an insulated mass,
The native bulwarks of the pass,
Huge as the tower which builders vain
Presumptuous piled on Shinar's plain.
The rocky summits, split and rent,
Formed turret, dome, or battlement,
Or seemed fantastically set
With cupola or minaret,
Wild crests as pagod ever decked,
Or mosque of Eastern architect.
Nor were these earth-born castles bare,
Nor lacked they many a banner fair;
For, from their shivered brows displayed,
Far o'er the unfathomable glade,
All twinkling with the dewdrops sheen,
The brier-rose fell in streamers green,
And creeping shrubs, of thousand dyes,
Waved in the west-wind's summer sighs.
Boon Nature scattered, free and wild,
Each plant or flower, the mountain's child.
Here eglantine embalmed the air,
Hawthorn and hazel mingled there;
The primrose pale and violet flower,
Found in each cliff a narrow bower;
Foxglove and nightshade, side by side,
Emblems of punishment and pride,
Grouped their dark hues with every stain
The weather-beaten crags retain.

With boughs that quaked at every breath,
Grey birch and aspen wept beneath ;
Aloft, the ash and warrior oak
Cast anchor in the rifted rock ;
And, higher yet, the pine-tree hung
His shattered trunk, and frequent flung,
Where seemed the cliffs to meet on high,
His boughs athwart the narrowed sky.
Highest of all, where white peaks glanced,
Where glist'ning streamers waved and danced,
The wanderer's eye could barely view
The summer heaven's delicious blue ;
So wondrous wild, the whole might seem
The scenery of a fairy dream."

The birches are nearly all gone. But the rest of this description is admirably true. Fitz-James, climbing the steep, and issuing
from the glen, looks down on the lake :—

" Where, gleaming with the setting sun,
One burnished sheet of living gold,
Loch Katrine lay beneath him rolled,
In all her length far winding lay,
With promontory, creek, and bay,
And islands that, empurpled bright,
Floated amid the livelier light,
And mountains, that like giants stand,
To sentinel enchanted land.
High on the south, huge Benvenue
Down on the lake in masses threw
Crags, knolls, and mounds, confus'dly hurled,
The fragments of an earlier world ;
A wildering forest feathered o'er
His ruined sides and summit hoar,
While on the north, through middle air,
Ben-an heaved high his forehead bare."

The tourist is now well out into the expanse of the lake, not very great at the most. Although some five hundred feet in depth, Loch Katrine is only a couple of miles in width at the broadest part, and its whole length from the Trossachs to the Stronachlachar Pier is under ten miles. The traveller who is able to walk should endeavour to take the road which runs along the northern shore. He will thus be able to follow Scott's descriptions much more nearly than from the deck of the steamer, which does not go very near the point at which Fitz-James is supposed to emerge from the woods and come in sight of the water. The road, or rather path—for it is impassable for carriages—brings us first to Ellen's Isle, which rises abruptly, covered with a thicket of dark foliage :—

> " The stranger viewed the shore around,
> 'Twas all so close with copsewood bound,
> Nor track nor pathway might declare
> That human foot frequented there,
> Until the mountain-maiden showed
> A clambering unsuspected road,
> That winded through the tangled screen,
> And opened on a narrow green,
> Where weeping birch and willow round
> With their long fibres swept the ground.
> Here, for retreat in dangerous hour,
> Some chief had framed a rustic bower.
>
> . . . .
>
> The wild-rose, eglantine, and broom,
> Wasted around their rich perfume ;
> The birch-trees wept in fragrant balm,
> The aspens slept beneath the calm ;
> The silver light, with quivering glance,
> Played on the water's still expanse,—
> Wild were the heart whose passions' sway
> Could rage beneath the sober ray !"

The southern shore of the lake is full of associations of a very similar character. The beautiful woods which clothe the foot of Benvenue afford innumerable opportunities for verifying and realising passages in this and other poems of Scott. Near the water's edge "is a very steep and most romantic hollow in the mountain of Benvenue, overhanging the south-eastern extremity of Loch Katrine. It is surrounded with stupendous rocks, and over-shadowed with birch-trees, mingled with oaks, the spontaneous production of the mountain, even where its cliffs appear denuded of soil. A dale in so wild a situation, and amid a people whose genius bordered on the romantic, did not remain without appropriate deities. The name literally implies the Corri, or Den, of the Wild or Shaggy Men. Perhaps this, as conjectured by Mr. Alex. Campbell, may have originally only implied its being the haunt of a ferocious banditti. But tradition has ascribed to the *Urisk*, who gives name to the cavern, a figure between a goat and a man ; in short, however much the classical reader may be startled, precisely that of the Grecian Satyr. The *Urisk* seems not to have inherited, with the form, the petulance of the sylvan deity of the classics : his occupation, on the contrary, resembled those of Milton's Lubbar Fiend, or of the Scottish Brownie, though he differed from both in name and appearance. 'The *Urisks*,' says Dr. Graham, 'were a set of lubberly supernaturals, who, like the Brownies, could be gained over by kind attention to perform the drudgery of the farm, and it was believed that many of the families in the High-lands had one of the order attached to it. They were supposed to be dispersed over the Highlands, each in his own wild recess, but the solemn stated meetings of the order were regularly held in this

Cave of Benvenue. This current superstition, no doubt, alludes to some circumstance in the ancient history of this country.'—*Scenery on the Southern Confines of Perthshire,* p. 19, 1806. It must be owned that the *Coir,* or Den, does not, in its present state, meet our ideas of a subterraneous grotto, or cave, being only a small and narrow cavity, among huge fragments of rocks rudely piled together. But such a scene is liable to convulsions of nature, which a Lowlander cannot estimate, and which may have choked up what was originally a cavern. At least the name and tradition warrant the author of a fictitious tale to assert its having been such at the remote period in which this scene is laid."

This passage is from the Notes to the *Lady of the Lake ;* but there is in reality no cave on the shore which would afford the slightest shelter, and a poetical licence of the largest kind must be allowed. The boatmen show travellers the only spot which at all approaches the description, but it is rather lower down than the foregoing passage would seem to indicate. Dr. Graham gives a more precise account :—

" After landing on the skirts of Benvenue, we reach the *Cave* (or more properly the *Cove) of the Goblins,* by a steep and narrow defile of a few hundred yards in length. It is a deep circular amphitheatre of at least six hundred yards of extent in its upper diameter, gradually narrowing towards the base, hemmed in all round by steep and towering rocks, and rendered impenetrable to the rays of the sun by a close covert of luxuriant trees. On the south and west it is bounded by the precipitous shoulder of Benvenue, to the height of at least five hundred feet ; towards the east, the rock appears at some former period to have tumbled down, strewing the whole course of its fall with immense fragments, which now serve only to give shelter to foxes, wild cats, and badgers."

But the poem itself gives a vivid picture of the surroundings of the spot :—

> " In Benvenue's most darksome cleft,
> A fair, though cruel, pledge was left;
> For Douglas, to his promise true,
> That morning from the isle withdrew
> And in a deep sequester'd dell
> Had sought a low and lonely cell.
> By many a bard, in Celtic tongue,
> Has Coir-nan Uriskin been sung;
> A softer name the Saxons gave,
> And called the grot the Goblin Cave.
> It was a wild and strange retreat,
> As e'er was trod by outlaw's feet.
> The dell, upon the mountain's crest,
> Yawned like a gash on warrior's breast;
> Its trench had staid full many a rock,
> Hurled by primeval earthquake shock
> From Benvenue's grey summit wild,
> And here, in random ruin piled,
> They frowned incumbent o'er the spot,
> And formed the rugged sylvan grot.
> The oak and birch, with mingled shade,
> At noontide there a twilight made,
> Unless when short and sudden shone
> Some straggling beam on cliff or stone.
> With such a glimpse as prophet's eye
> Gains on thy depth, Futurity.
> No murmur waked the solemn still,
> Save tinkling of a fountain rill ;
> But when the wind chafed with the lake,
> A sullen sound would upward break,

With dashing hollow voice, that spoke
The incessant war of wave and rock.
Suspended cliffs, with hideous sway,
Seemed nodding o'er the cavern grey.
From such a den the wolf had sprung,
In such the wild cat leaves her young ;
Yet Douglas and his daughter fair
Sought for a space their safety there.
Grey Superstition's whisper dread
Debarred the spot to vulgar tread ;
For there, she said, did fays resort,
And satyrs hold their sylvan court,
By moonlight tread their mystic maze,
And blast the rash beholder's gaze."

Above the Goblin's Cave, higher up the face of Benvenue, is
the pass called in the poem, Beal-nam-bo, or, in full, Bealach-nam-
bo, "The Cattle Pass." It is to be feared that in the old cateran
days Ellen's Isle was a place for the concealment of cattle stolen
from the Lowlands, and perhaps a "cattle-pen, shambles, and
larder," all in one. The clan Macgregor drove their booty to this
place of refuge from the Lowlands beyond Loch Lomond by the
pass of Bealach-nam-bo, the only practicable road between Benvenue itself and the water's edge. It is now visited by the
traveller with a very different purpose, for it affords some of the
grandest scenery in the whole district. From a shoulder of the
mountain, perhaps a thousand feet above the level of the lake, the
view is most charming. Few of us have seen it at sunrise, and it
may even be questioned whether Scott himself had ever witnessed
what he so vividly paints in these lines from the beginning of the
third canto :—

" The summer dawn's reflected hue
To purple changed Loch Katrine blue;
Mildly and soft the western breeze
Just kissed the lake, just stirred the trees,
And the pleased lake, like maiden coy,
Trembled but dimpled not for joy;
The mountain-shadows on her breast
Were neither broken nor at rest;
In bright uncertainty they lie,
Like future joys to Fancy's eye.
The water-lily to the light
Her chalice reared of silver bright;
The doe awoke, and to the lawn,
Begemmed with dew-drops, led her fawn;
The grey mist left the mountain side,
The torrent showed its glistening pride;
Invisible in fleckèd sky,
The lark sent down her revelry;
The blackbird and the speckled thrush .
Good-morrow gave from brake and bush;
In answer coo'd the cushat dove
Her notes of peace, and rest, and love."

Such a scene, at such an hour, must often have passed unheeded before the eyes of the wild Macgregors as they drove the herds of their Lowland neighbours through Beal-nam-bo to their fastness on Loch Katrine. Rob Roy himself, who may be called the last of the caterans, had his headquarters not far off. For this was the Macgregor's country, and here they were more than once almost exterminated; yet somehow the clan, after repeated proscriptions, has managed to survive, and to be pretty numerous still. . A terrible clan-battle was that between the Macgregors and Colquhouns, which took place in this district, at Glenfruin, early in the seventeenth century, and resulted indirectly in the temporary ruin of the Macgregors, although they were victorious in the fight itself. Some of the authorities attribute to them the murder of the chief of Luss after the battle in cold blood, while others say that it was perpetrated at a later period, and by the Macfarlanes. At Glenfruin, however, two hundred of the Colquhouns were left dead on the field, while only two of the Macgregors were slain. Scott says (Notes to the *Lady of the Lake*) :—

"The consequences of the battle of Glenfruin were very calamitous to the family of Macgregor, who had already been considered as an unruly clan. The widows of the slain Colquhouns—sixty, it is said, in number—appeared in doleful procession before the king at Stirling, each riding upon a white palfrey, and bearing in her hand the bloody shirt of her husband displayed upon a pike. James VI. was so much moved by the complaints of this 'choir of mourning dames,' that he let loose his vengeance against the Macgregors, without either bounds or moderation. The very name of the clan was proscribed, and those by whom it had been borne were given up to sword and fire, and absolutely hunted down by bloodhounds like wild beasts. Argyle and the Campbells on the one hand, Montrose, with the Grahames and Buchanans, on the other, are said to have been the chief instruments in suppressing this devoted clan. The Laird of Macgregor surrendered to the former, on condition that he would take him out of Scottish ground. But, to use Birrel's expression, he kept 'a Highlandman's promise;' and, although he fulfilled his word to the letter, by carrying him as far as Berwick, he afterwards brought him back to Edinburgh, where he was executed with eighteen of his clan.

(Birrel's *Diary*, 2nd Oct., 1603.) The clan Gregor being thus driven to utter despair, seem to have renounced the laws from the benefit of which they were excluded, and their depredations produced new Acts of Council, confirming the severity of their proscription, which had only the effect of rendering them still more united and desperate. It is a most extraordinary proof of the ardent and invincible spirit of clanship, that, notwithstanding the repeated proscriptions providently ordained by the legislature, ' for the *timeous preventing* the disorders and oppression that may fall out by the said name and clan of Macgregors, and their followers,' they were in 1715 and 1745 a potent clan, and continue to subsist as a distinct and numerous race."

The part which they played in these later transactions and others form the subjects of at least two other romances by Scott, who seems to have had a peculiar interest in the history of these " Children of the. Mist," as they were called. After existing for centuries in a chronic state of rebellion, and after repeated Acts of Parliament had been passed forbidding them even to use their ancient surname, the dawn of a more civilised age found them still numerous, though dispersed ; and in 1822 the penal enactments were finally removed. On the passing of the relaxation and the reversal of the outlawry, no fewer than eight hundred and twenty-six persons were found anxious to resume their patronymic ; and by a solemn deed, which they all subscribed, to acknowledge Sir John Murray, Bart., as the chief of the clan. He thereupon assumed the name which had belonged to his ancestors, by Royal licence, and was formally admitted to all the barren honours of the chieftainship.

KILCHURN CASTLE.

O N Loch Awe we are in the heart of the Campbell's country. For a hundred miles the lands of Breadalbane stretch, from Rannoch to the sea ; then Argyll takes up the tale, and continues it away into the Islands. Before the Campbells came, these were the fastnesses of many wild, but scarcely wilder tribes. The Macgregors and the Macdougals made the saying, "It's a far cry to Loch Awe," something more than a mere geographical expression. When the Lowlander's herd was once safe over the mountains, he might never hope to see it again. The robbers went unpunished, and remained hidden till another opportunity occurred for a raid on their richer neighbours. All this is now changed. There are still Macdougals and Macgregors as well as Campbells by the banks of Loch Awe. They may say, in the words of Scott,

> " Glen Orchy's proud mountains, Caolchuirn and her towers,
> Glen Strae and Glen Lyon no longer are ours."

But they are not wholly landless, and the representative in the male line of the ancient Lords of Lorn is still in the neighbour-hood. As to the robbery of Southerns, it is carried on under legalised forms. The Highlander now puts his demands upon paper ; but, instead of fleeing to Loch Awe, he is able to attract

the Lowlander to visit him among his mountains, and to prove how far a cry it is by personal experience.

Loch Awe and Ben Cruachan figured in history before Kilchurn was built. Sir Walter Scott alludes to the story of Bruce's expedition to Argyleshire in his *Highland Widow;* but the following account occurs in the Notes to the *Lord of the Isles :*—

" The Lord of Lorn, who flourished during the wars of Bruce, was Allaster (or Alexander) Macdougal, called Allaster of Argyle. He had married the third daughter of John, called the Red Comyn, who was slain by Bruce in the Dominican Church at Dumfries ; and hence he was a mortal enemy of that prince, and more than once reduced him to great straits during the early and distressed period of his reign, as we shall have repeated occasion to notice. Bruce, when he began to obtain an ascendancy in Scotland, took the first opportunity in his power to requite these injuries. He marched into Argyleshire to lay waste the country. John of Lorn, son of the chieftain, was posted with his followers in the formidable pass between Dalmally and Bunawe. It is a narrow path along the verge of the huge and precipitous mountain called Cruachan-Ben, and guarded on the other side by a precipice overhanging Loch Awe. The pass seems to the eye of a soldier as strong, as it is wild and romantic to that of an ordinary traveller. But the skill of Bruce had anticipated this difficulty. While his main body, engaged in a skirmish with the men of Lorn, detained their attention to the front of their position, James of Douglas, with Sir Alexander Fraser, Sir William Wiseman, and Sir Andrew Grey, ascended the mountain with a select body of archery, and obtained possession of the heights which commanded the pass. A volley of arrows descending upon them directly warned the Argyleshire men of their perilous situation ; and their resistance, which had hitherto been bold and manly, was changed into a precipitate flight. The deep and rapid river of Awe was then (we learn the fact from Barbour with some surprise) crossed by a bridge. This bridge the mountaineers attempted to demolish, but Bruce's followers were too close upon their rear ; they were therefore without refuge and defence, and were dispersed with great slaughter. John of Lorn, suspicious of the event, had early betaken himself to the galleys which he had upon the lake; but the feelings which Barbour assigns to him, while witnessing the rout and slaughter of his followers, exculpate him from the charge of cowardice.

> ' To Jhone off Lorne it suld displese
> I trow, quhen he his men mycht se,
> Owte off his schippis fra the se,
> Be slayne and chassyt in the hill,
> That he mycht set na help thar till.
> Bot it angrys als gretumly,
> To gud hartis that are worthi,
> To se thar fayis fulfill thair will
> As to thaim selff to thole the ill.'

B. VII., v. 394.

After this decisive engagement, Bruce laid waste Argyleshire, and besieged Dunstaffnage Castle, on the western shore of Lorn, compelled it to surrender, and placed in the principal stronghold of the Macdougals a garrison and governor of his own. The elder Macdougal, now wearied with the contest, submitted to the victor ; but his son, ' rebellious,' says Barbour, ' as he wont to be,' fled to England by sea. When the wars between the Bruce and Baliol factions again broke out in the reign of David II., the

Lords of Lorn were again found upon the losing side, owing to their hereditary enmity to the house of Bruce. Accordingly, upon the issue of that contest, they were deprived by David II. and his successor of by far the greater part of their extensive territories, which were conferred upon Stewart, called the Knight of Lorn."

In another passage of the same book, Scott further writes :—

"Robert Bruce, after his defeat at Methven, being hard pressed by the English, endeavoured, with the dispirited remnant of his followers, to escape from Breadalbane and the mountains of Perthshire into the Argyleshire Highlands. But he was encountered and repulsed, after a very severe engagement, by the Lord of Lorn. Bruce's personal strength and courage were never displayed to greater advantage than in this conflict. There is a tradition in the family of the Macdougals of Lorn, that their chieftain engaged in personal battle with Bruce himself, while the latter was employed in protecting the retreat of his men ; that Macdougal was struck down by the king, whose strength of body was equal to his vigour of mind, and would have been slain on the spot, had not two of Lorn's vassals, a father and son, whom tradition terms Mackeoch, rescued him, by seizing the mantle of the monarch, and dragging him from above his adversary. Bruce rid himself of these foes by two blows of his redoubted battle-axe, but was so closely pressed by the other followers of Lorn, that he was forced to abandon the mantle, and brooch which fastened it, clasped in the dying grasp of the Mackeochs. A studded brooch, said to have been that which King Robert lost upon this occasion, was long preserved in the family of Macdougal, and was lost in a fire which consumed their temporary residence."

Bruce died in 1329, and in 1440, during the reign of his descendant, James II., the earliest portion of the existing remains of Kilchurn Castle was built by Sir Duncan Campbell.

It stands on a space of level land close to the lake, and consists, besides the main building, of northern and southern wings, added as late as 1615. It is well described in a charming volume—the *Painter's Camp*—by the accomplished Philip Gilbert Hamerton, from which we borrow the accompanying illustration.

He says (p. 171):—" One bright evening, late in September, I set out, after dinner, for Kilchurn, to get a series of observations on moonlight colour; for I had studied Kilchurn closely enough to remember the ordinary daylight colour of every part of it. . . When we got to Kilchurn, and had safely passed the bar at the entrance to the bay, we floated quietly out into the midst, and Kilchurn stood before us in the full mellow light of the moon. . . The old castle, like most old buildings, has been ruined by man, not by time. Henry the Eighth, Oliver Cromwell, blundering stewards, and apathetic proprietors, are the real authors of most of the ruins in Britain. With a little friendly care and attention a strong building will last a thousand years, but a fool will demolish it in a day. Kilchurn is a ruin, merely because an economical steward thought the roof timber would come in very well for the new castle at Taymouth, and so carried it thither. But he had omitted to measure the beams, which turned out to be too short, and therefore, of course, useless. Then when the roof was off, the old castle became a general stone quarry, and furnished stones ready cut to all the farmers who chose to steal them. And the new inn at Dalmally, and the queer little sham Gothic church over the bridge, being erected some time afterwards, the now ruined castle furnished hewn stones to both those edifices. There is not a fragment of wood in all Kilchurn; there is not one step left there of all its winding stairs. Yet in the '45' the building was garrisoned against the Prince; and in the latter end of the last century there were tapestry on the walls and wine in the cellar, and a casque and shirt of mail still hung on the walls of the armoury. Alone with these relics lingered one old servant as housekeeper. She was the last inhabitant. Some domestics might have objected to the situation. Fancy a London housekeeper shut up alone in a great ghostly feudal castle on a narrow island rock, with waves roaring round it in the long northern winter nights, and the sobbing wind flapping the figured tapestry, and rattling the armour in the armoury."

Mr. Hamerton has spent much time at Loch Awe, and is, as a descriptive writer of the first class, the best guide to its beauties. He has not been content to celebrate its charms in prose alone. *The Isles of Loch Awe* is a volume full of poetical beauty and power, and a charming pocket companion in this part of the Highlands. We must return to it presently for a legend of the place, but pause meanwhile at the name of one whom Mr. Hamerton will allow us to call a greater poet. Wordsworth visited Scotland in 1803 and 1814, and a third time in 1833. The record of his journeys has lately been published, and we venture to quote the following passage, adding in full the poem of which the first three lines only are given in *Miss Wordsworth's Journal* (p. 139):—

"When we had ascended half-way up the hill, directed by the man, I took a nearer footpath, and at the top came in view of a most impressive scene—a ruined castle on an island almost in the middle of the last compartment of the lake, backed by a mountain cove, down which came a roaring stream. The castle occupied every foot of the island that was visible to us, appearing to rise out of the water; mists rested upon the mountain side, with spots of sunshine between; there was a mild desolation in the low grounds, a solemn grandeur in the mountains, and the castle was wild, yet stately—not dismantled of its turrets, nor the walls broken down, though completely in ruin. After having stood some minutes, I joined William on the high road; and both wishing to stay longer near this place, we requested the man to drive his little boy on to

Dalmally, about two miles further, and leave the car at the inn. He told us that the ruin was called Kilchurn Castle; that it belonged to Lord Breadalbane, and had been built by one of the ladies of that family for her defence during her lord's absence at the Crusades, for which purpose she levied a tax of seven years' rent upon her tenants :* he said that from that side of the lake it did not appear, in very dry weather, to stand upon an island; but that it was possible to go over to it without being wet-shod. We were very lucky in seeing it after a great flood; for its enchanting effect was chiefly owing to its situation in the lake—a decayed palace rising out of the plain of waters! I have called it a palace, for such feeling it gave to me, though having been built as a place of defence—a castle, or fortress. We turned again and re-ascended the hill, and sate a long time in the middle of it, looking on the castle and the huge mountain cove opposite; and William, addressing himself to the ruin, poured out these verses :—

> " Child of loud-throated War! the mountain Stream
> Roars in thy hearing; but thy hour of rest
> Is come, and thou art silent in thy age;
> Save when the wind sweeps by and sounds are caught
> Ambiguous, neither wholly thine nor theirs.
> Oh! there is life that breathes not; Powers there are
> That touch each other to the quick in modes
> Which the gross world no sense hath to perceive,
> No soul to dream of. What art thou, from care
> Cast off—abandoned by thy rugged Sire,
> Nor by soft Peace adopted; though, in place
> And in dimension, such that thou might'st seem
> But a mere footstool to yon sovereign Lord,

* Not very probable.

Huge Cruachan (a thing that meaner hills
Might crush, nor know that it had suffered harm);
Yet he, not loth, in favour of thy claims
To reverence, suspends his own; submitting
All that the God of Nature hath conferred,
All that he holds in common with the stars,
To the memorial majesty of Time
Impersonated in thy calm decay!

Take, then, thy seat, Vicegerent unreproved!
Now, while a farewell gleam of evening light
Is fondly lingering on thy shattered front,
Do thou, in turn, be paramount; and rule
Over the pomp and beauty of a scene
Whose mountains, torrents, lake, and woods unite
To pay thee homage; and with these are joined,
In willing admiration and respect,
Two Hearts, which in thy presence might be called
Youthful as Spring.—Shade of departed Power,
Skeleton of unfleshed humanity,
The chronicle were welcome that should call
Into the compass of distinct regard
The toils and struggles of thy infant years!
Yon foaming flood seems motionless as ice;
Its dizzy turbulence eludes the eye,
Frozen by distance; so, majestic Pile,
To the perception of this Age, appear
Thy fierce beginnings, softened and subdued
And quieted in character—the strife,
The pride, the fury uncontrollable,
Lost on the aërial heights of the Crusades!"

This last line refers to a legend which Mr. Hamerton has made
the subject of a poem on Kilchurn. We venture to quote a few
lines, but our readers must look for the complete story, of which

this is the commencement, in the book itself (p. 39). Mr. Hamerton says :—

> " Sir Colin Campbell was a knight of Rhodes.
> For seven years he risked continually .
> His life in foreign warfare. Seven years
> Waited the Lady Margaret, his wife,
> Like a poor widow, living sparingly,
> And saving all the produce of his lands
> To build an island fortress on Loch Awe,
> There to receive Sir Colin, and so prove
> Her thrift and duty. Little more we know
> Of what she did to occupy her time :
> Perhaps a narrow but perpetual round ·
> Of mean and servile duties, too obscure
> To be recorded, kept her nerves in health.
> And truly it is well to handle life
> Not daintily. The best resource in grief
> Is downright labour. This at least we know,
> That the good spouse of that brave Highland chief
> Looked to her husband's interest and hers,
> When from her quarries silently—before
> Loud blasting tore the layers of the rock—
> The clansmen ferried loads of idle stones
> Across the water ; and on what was then
> An island, and is yet in winter floods,
> Made them most useful servants—trusty guards
> Of all the treasure of a Highland chief—
> His wife, his tail, his cattle, and his goods."

Scott has not unfrequently made passing allusions to Loch Awe ; but Kilchurn figures under another name in his *Legend of Montrose.* As Mr. Hamerton says :—

> " This is Sir Walter's pile of Ardenvohr,
> Changed since Dalgetty criticised its strength."

The whole scene is too amusing, and has become too famous now
to be omitted here; but the judicious reader may perceive that it
will not exactly fit in all particulars what even in its ruins Kilchurn
professed to be. Sir Walter rather magnifies it :—

" 'This house of yours, now, Sir Duncan, is a very pretty defeu-
sible sort of a tenement, and yet it is hardly such as a cavaliero of
honour would expect to maintain his credit by holding out for
many days. For, Sir Duncan, if it pleases you to notice, your
house is overcrowed, and slighted, or commanded, as we military
men say, by yonder round hillock to the landward, whereon an
enemy might stell such a battery of cannon as would make ye glad
to beat a chamade within forty-eight hours, unless it pleased the
Lord extraordinarily to shew mercy.'

" 'There is no road,' replied Sir Duncan, somewhat shortly,
'by which cannon can be brought against Ardenvohr. The
swamps and morasses around my house would scarce carry your
horse and yourself, excepting by such paths as could be rendered
impassable within a few hours.'

" 'Sir Duncan,' said the Captain, 'it is your pleasure to
suppose so; and yet we martial men say, that where there is a
sea-coast there is always a naked side, seeing that cannon and
munition, where they cannot be transported by land, may be right
easily brought by sea near to the place where they are to be put in
action. Neither is a castle, however secure in its situation, to be
accounted altogether invincible, or, as they say, impregnable ; for
I protest t'ye, Sir Duncan, that I have known twenty-five men, by
the mere surprise and audacity of the attack, win, at point of
pike, as strong a hold as this of Ardenvohr, and put to the sword,

captivate, or hold to the ransom, the defenders, being ten times their own number.'

"Notwithstanding Sir Duncan Campbell's knowledge of the world, and his power of concealing his internal emotion, he appeared piqued and hurt at these reflections, which the Captain made with the most unconscious gravity, having merely selected the subject of conversation as one upon which he thought himself capable of shining, and, as they say, of laying down the law, without exactly recollecting that the topic might not be equally agreeable to his landlord.

"'To cut this matter short,' said Sir Duncan, with an expression of voice and countenance somewhat agitated, 'it is unnecessary for you to tell me, Captain Dalgetty, that a castle may be stormed if it is not valorously defended, or surprised if it is not heedfully watched. I trust this poor house of mine will not be found in any of these predicaments, should even Captain Dalgetty himself choose to beleaguer it.'

"'For all that, Sir Duncan,' answered the persevering commander, 'I would premonish you, as a friend, to trace out a sconce upon that round hill, with a good graffe, or ditch, whilk may be easily accomplished by compelling the labour of the boors in the vicinity; it being the custom of the valorous Gustavus Adolphus to fight as much by the spade and shovel, as by sword, pike, and musket. Also, I would advise you to fortify the said sconce, not only by a foussie, or graffe, but also by certain stackets, or palisades.'—(Here Sir Duncan, becoming impatient, left the apartment, the Captain following him to the door, and raising his voice as he retreated, until he was fairly out of hearing.)—'The whilk stackets, or palisades, should be artificially framed with re-entering angles and loopholes, or crenelles, for musketry, whereof it shall arise that the foemen —— The Highland brute! the old Highland brute! They are as proud as peacocks, and as obstinate as tups, and here he has missed an opportunity of making his house as pretty an irregular fortification as an invading army ever broke their teeth upon. But I see,' he continued, looking down from the window upon the bottom of the precipice, 'they have got Gustavus safe ashore. Proper fellow! I would know that toss of his head among a whole squadron. I must go to see what they are to make of him.'

.   .   .   .

" He had no sooner reached, however, the court to the seaward, and put himself in the act of descending the staircase, than two Highland sentinels, advancing their Lochaber axes, gave him to understand that this was a service of danger.

" 'Diavolo,' said the soldier, 'and I have got no pass-word. I could not speak a syllable of their salvage gibberish, an' it were to save me from the provost-marshal.'

" 'I will be your surety, Captain Dalgetty,' said Sir Duncan, who had again approached him without his observing from whence; 'and we will go together, and see how your favourite charger is accommodated.'

" He conducted him accordingly down the staircase to the beach, and from thence by a short turn behind a large rock, which concealed the stables and other offices belonging to the castle. Captain Dalgetty became sensible, at the same time, that the side of the castle to the land was rendered totally inaccessible by a ravine, partly natural and partly scarped with great care and labour, so as to be only passed by a drawbridge. Still, however, the Captain insisted, notwithstanding the triumphant air with which Sir Duncan pointed out his defences, that a sconce should be erected on Drumsnab, the round eminence to the east of the castle, in respect the house might be annoyed from thence by burning bullets full of fire, shot out of cannon, according to the curious invention of Stephen Bathian, King of Poland, whereby that Prince utterly ruined the great Muscovite city of Moscow. This invention, Captain Dalgetty owned, he had not yet witnessed; but observed 'that it would give him particular delectation to witness the same put to the proof against Ardenvohr, or any other castle of similar strength;' observing, 'that so curious an experiment could not but afford the greatest delight to all admirers of the military art.'"

The point of view chosen by our artist is on the eastern shore of the loch, looking towards Ben Loy, which raises its tall head beyond and above the castle. Dalmally, the usual resting-place of tourists, is about half-way between the castle and the mountain, and from it, as a base of operations, the ascent of Ben Cruachan is most easily made. There are few such views in Scotland as that to be had on a clear day from the summit. Although some six or seven hundred feet lower than Ben Nevis, the situation of Ben Cruachan affords a nearer sight of the beautiful islands of the west, the bay of Oban, and even—beyond " the sandy Coll" and the "wild Tiree"—the distant hills of Rum and Skye. To the north and east, Loch Etive and Glencoe, Glen Strae and Glen Orchy, seem just beneath our feet; while farther into the blue

distance all the mountains of the Scottish Highlands roll wave
after wave of solid rock towards the German Ocean. Again we
have recourse to Scott for the expression of feelings almost unutter-
able in the presence of such scenes :—

> " Stranger! if e'er thine ardent step hath traced
>   The northern realms of ancient Caledon,
>   Where the proud Queen of Wilderness hath placed,
>   By lake and cataract, her lonely throne ;
>   Sublime but sad delight thy soul hath known,
>   Gazing on pathless glen and mountain high,
>   Listing where from the cliffs the torrents thrown
>   Mingle their echoes with the eagle's cry,
> And with the sounding lake, and with the moaning sky.

> " Yes! 'twas sublime, but sad. The loneliness
>   Loaded thy heart, the desert tired thine eye ;
>   And strange and awful fears began to press
>   Thy bosom with a stern solemnity.
>   Then hast thou wished some woodman's cottage nigh,
>   Something that showed of life, though low and mean ;
>   Glad sight, its curling wreath of smoke to spy,
>   Glad sound, its cock's blithe carol would have been,
> Or children whooping wild beneath the willows green.

> " Such are the scenes, where savage grandeur wakes
>   An awful thrill that softens into sighs ;
>   Such feelings rouse them by dim Rannoch's lakes,
>   In dark Glencoe such gloomy raptures rise :
>   Or farther, where, beneath the northern skies,
>   Chides wild Loch-Eribol his caverns hoar—
>   But, be the minstrel judge, they yield the prize
>   Of desert dignity to that dread shore,
> That sees grim Coolin rise, and hears Coriskin roar."

BEN NEVIS.

THERE is always a feeling of disappointment excited by the first sight of a place of which we have heard much. The traveller who sets out from Salisbury for Stonehenge, and ascends the long succession of dusty chalk hills in the blinding glare of the summer sun, can hardly believe his eyes when, slowly toiling up one more "down," he suddenly sees the object of all his trouble on the grassy slope before him. It is just far enough from the road not to look great, and just near enough to be recognised with a certainty which would willingly think itself deceived. The case is the same with remarkable objects of natural scenery. The Giants' Causeway, for example, and even Niagara, do not strike the beholder at first sight. They need to be examined, to be measured, to be compared, mentally, with other objects, before their vastness, their strangeness, their real pre-eminence is discerned.

Of no place in the whole of the three kingdoms is this more true than of Ben Nevis. The tallest mountain in England is Scawfell, with its three thousand one hundred and sixty feet, but Ben Nevis is more than a thousand feet higher. Snowdon is the

highest peak of Wales, but Ben Nevis is eight hundred feet
higher. Carrantuohill, in Kerry, exceeds all other Irish hills,
but Ben Nevis is nine hundred feet higher. Yet it may safely be
asserted, that any one who has seen them all would have thought,
apart from ascertained measurements, that Ben Nevis was less than
the least.

Much of this feeling is caused by the absence of anything like a
peak or point to mark the summit. Ben Nevis has no single point,
but three ridges at the top are of nearly equal height, and it thus
presents a rounded aspect to the spectator below. The great mass,
and, so to speak, the weight of the whole mountain is sufficiently
grand and striking; but this is a thing of which the eye alone can
hardly judge. When the traveller wakens up the morning after his
arrival at Fort-William, he hastens to take a look at the highest
mountain in Great Britain; but it is not by its height that he is
first impressed. It is massive, great, even magnificent; but compared with Ben Lomond, or Moel Siabad, far from beautiful.
After a little this feeling of disappointment subsides, and a climb
to the top is amply rewarded by a most extensive view over some
of the loveliest scenery in Scotland.

Perhaps the best account of Ben Nevis will be found in the
Scenery and Geology of Scotland, by Mr. Geikie, of Edinburgh.
He says (p. 99) :—

"If one would grasp at once the leading features of Highland
scenery, let him betake himself to some mountain-top that
stands a little apart from its neighbours, and looks over them
into the wilds beyond. A better height could not be chosen than
the summit of Ben Nevis. None other rises more majestically

above the surrounding hills, or looks over a wider sweep of mountain and moor, glen and corry, lake and firth, far away to the islands that lie amid the western sea. In no other place is the general and varied character of the Highlands better illustrated; and from none can the geologist, whose eye is open to the changes wrought by sub-aërial waste on the surface of the country, gain a more vivid insight into their reality and magnitude. To this, as a typical and easily accessible locality, I shall have occasion to refer more than once. Let the reader, in the meantime, imagine himself sitting by the side of the grey cairn on the highest peak of the British Isles, watching the shadows of an autumnal sky stealing over the vast sea of mountains that lies spread out as in a map around him. And while no sound falls upon his ear, save now and then a fitful moaning of the wind among the snow-drifts of the dark precipice below, let him try to analyse some of the chief elements of the landscape. It is easy to recognise the more marked heights and hollows. To the south, away down Loch Linnhe, he can see the hills of Mull and the Paps of Jura closing in the horizon. Westwards, Loch Eil seems to lie at his feet, winding up into the lonely mountains, yet filled twice a-day with the tides of the salt sea. Far over the hills, beyond the head of the loch, he looks across Arisaig, and can see the cliffs of the Isle of Eigg, and the dark peaks of Rum, with the Atlantic gleaming below them. Further to the north-west the blue line of the Cuchullins rises along the sky-line, and then, sweeping over all the intermediate ground, through Arisaig and Knoydart and Clanranald's country, mountain rises beyond mountain, ridge beyond ridge, cut through by dark glens, and varied here and there with the sheen of lake and tarn. Northward runs the mysterious line of the Great Glen, with its chain of lochs. Thence to east and south the same billowy sea of mountain-tops stretches out as far as eye can follow it—the hills and glens of Lochaber, the wide green strath of Spean, the grey corries of Glen Trieg and Glen Nevis, the distant sweep of the moors and mountains of Brae Lyon and the Perthshire Highlands, the spires of Glen Coe, and thence round again to the blue waters of Loch Linnhe.

"In musing over this wide panorama, the observer cannot fail to note that while there are everywhere local peculiarities in the outline of the hills, and the shapes of the sides of the valleys, there is yet a general uniformity of contour over the whole. What seem at a nearer view rough craggy peaks and pinnacles, seen from this height are dwarfed into mere minor irregularities of surface. And thus over the whole of the wide landscape one mountain-ridge appears after another, with the same large features, rising and sinking from glen to glen with the same smoothed summits, broken now and again where from some hidden valley a circular corry or craggy cliff lifts itself bare to the sun."

The impossibility of mere words to paint a landscape has often been insisted upon, but if it be within a writer's power to make a view visible without the artist's aid, Mr. Geikie has contrived to accomplish the task. The same descriptive pen has exercised itself in an account of the ascent of Ben Nevis (p. 116) :—

"If the observer be sure of foot and steady of eye, let him ascend that mountain, not by the regular track, but up the long

and almost equally lofty ridge which lies to the east, and thence
along the narrow and somewhat perilous 'col' which circles round
to the southern front of the great Ben. The ascent lies first among
heathery slopes, channelled with brooks of clear cold water, and
roughened with grey, worn, and weathered hummocks of schist and
granite. Blocks of granite of every size cumber the ground,
standing sometimes on rocky knolls, and sometimes half buried in
morass. That the frosts of many a century have been busy here,
is shown by the countless boulders and protruding knobs of rock
which have been split open along their joints. Slanting up the
mountain, the observer has leisure to remark, as he crosses
streamlet after streamlet, that their channels, sometimes cut
deeply into the solid rock, are evidently the work of the running
water. He finds them grow fewer as he rises. On the slopes, too,
the boggy peat and shaggy heather begin to give way to long
streams of angular granite blocks, among which the scanty vegeta-
tion is at last reduced to mere scattered patches of short grass and
moss, with here and there a little Alpine plant. A wilderness of
débris now covers the bald scalp of the mountain. The solid
granite itself cannot be seen through the depths of its own
accumulated fragments; but when the crest of the height is gained,
the rock is found peering in shattered fragments from amidst the
ruin. This narrow mountain-ridge is then seen to rise between
two profound glens. That to the north-east is crowned by a
rampart-like range of pink-hued granite cliffs; from which long
courses of *débris* descend to the bottom. The glen that lies far
below on the south-west is overhung on its further side by the vast
rugged precipice of Ben Nevis, rising some fifteen hundred or two

thousand feet above the stream that wanders through the gloom at its base. That dark wall of porphyry can now be seen from bottom to top, with its huge masses of rifted rock standing up like ample buttresses into the light, and its deep recesses and clefts, into which the summer sun never reaches, and where the winter snow never melts. . . . So narrow is the edge of the ridge in some places, that a single block of granite may split into two parts, of which one would roll crashing down the steep slope into the valley on the left hand, while the other would leap to the bottom of the glen on the right. In this sharp form the ridge divides, one arm sweeping round the head of the glen on the north-east side, while the other circles westwards to the shoulders of Ben Nevis."

These glens, of which Mr. Geikie has much more to say, afford another point of interest beyond those on which he speaks so eloquently. The snow which never melts, as he says in the above passage, is the subject of a curious local usage. Cameron of Glen Nevis holds his lands from the Crown by the tenure of presenting, when required, a snowball to the Queen at midsummer, or at any other time it is asked for. The Camerons muster strongly in the neighbourhood of Ben Nevis. Fassifern and Lochiel are both close by—to the west, and near them is the monument of Prince Charles, erected to commemorate his landing in 1745, when, on the 19th August, his standard was here first displayed by Tullibardine, in the presence of a thousand Highlanders, chiefly of the Cameron clan. At Kilmallie, which lies close to Ben Nevis, but across the lake, and facing Fort-William, is the monument of Colonel Cameron of the 92nd Highlanders, who was killed at Quatre Bras. Though the epitaph on the monument was written by Sir Walter Scott, and though the hero's father was made a baronet in consideration of his son's great services and death, the lines of Byron will form a more lasting memorial of him, and one better known to English readers. They occur in *Childe Harold*, Canto III., when, having alluded to the famous ball at Brussels, and to the fall of "Brunswick's fated chieftain," he goes on :—

> "And wild and high the 'Cameron's gathering' rose !
> The war-note of Lochiel, which Albyn's hills
> Have heard, and heard, too, have her Saxon foes :—
> How in the noon of night that pibroch thrills,
> Savage and shrill ! But with the breath that fills
> Their mountain pipe, so fill the mountaineers
> With the fierce native daring which instils
> The stirring memory of a thousand years—
> And Evan's, Donald's fame rings in each clansman's ears.

> "And Ardennes waves above them her green leaves,
> Dewy with Nature's tear-drops as they pass—
> Grieving, if aught inanimate e'er grieves,
> Over the unreturning brave—alas !
> Ere evening to be trodden like the grass
> Which now beneath them, but above shall grow
> In its next verdure, when this fiery mass
> Of living valour, rolling on the foe,
> And burning with high hope, shall moulder cold and low."

The Camerons of Fassifern were descended from John Cameron, the second son of John Cameron of Lochiel, who, having been out in 1715, was attainted, and forfeited his lands. Lochiel had two other sons ; the elder, Donald, was the Lochiel who figured in the

'45 ; and the younger, Alexander, a medical man, was himself the hero of as sad a tragedy as any with which the family name is connected. He was at Culloden, where he succoured indifferently both friends and foes, and ministered as a surgeon to the wounds of the soldiers of both parties. Finding himself still deeply implicated, like his brother, in the rebellion, he fled to Flanders, where his father lived ; but returning to Scotland in 1753, more than eight years after the rising, he was arrested, and sent to London, where he was imprisoned in the Savoy, brought to trial, and put to death. His body was buried in the ancient chapel of St. John, in the Savoy ; and a stained-glass window, erected with the special leave of the Queen by his present representatives, marks at once the sadness of his fate and the improvement in manners, which would render such an act of barbarous justice impossible at the present day.

John Cameron of Fassifern, the brother of this ill-fated individual, was the father of Ewen Campbell, created a baronet, as we have said, in recognition of the services of his eldest son, who perished at Quatre Bras. Lochiel was also represented in this glorious campaign. His eldest son, the late chief, was in the Grenadier Guards at Waterloo. These modern Camerons were, however, only worthy sons of their great ancestor, " Evan Dhu," whose history forms so strange, yet so characteristic, an episode in the history of Scotland. To give an accurate idea of the state of society there in the time of Cromwell and the Civil Wars, a notice of him would be most useful ; and, as his life was passed under the shadow of Ben Nevis, a short account of it will not be out of place here. Ewen Cameron of Lochiel was born in 1629—that is, in the fourth year of the reign of Charles the First—and died in 1719, more than five years after the accession of the House of Hanover. He thus lived through some of the most stirring scenes, and took part in many of the events, of that disturbed era. The clan had originally been seated on the eastern side of the loch, where they held their lands under the Lord of the Isles. They were divided into three families or septs, and in 1431, when Donald Dhu invaded Scotland, they were attacked and dispersed by him, and their chief driven away into Ireland. In 1564, Queen Mary granted a charter confirming Donald Cameron of "Lochyell" in his estates on the western side of the lakes, and these lands descended duly to his grandson "Evan Dhu." This chieftain was a staunch Royalist, and in 1652 he joined the Scottish rising against Cromwell, which General Monk endeavoured fruitlessly to suppress. At last a kind of truce was concluded, in which Lochiel received very honourable terms. But Sir Walter Scott's account of the matter is the best : we read in the *Tales of a Grandfather* (chap. xlvi.) :—

"It was the constant policy of Cromwell and his officers, both in Ireland and Scotland, to cut down and destroy the forests in which the insurgent natives found places of defence and conceal-ment. In conformity with this general rule, the commandant of Inverlochy embarked three hundred men in two light-armed vessels, with directions to disembark at a place called Achdalew, for the purpose of destroying Lochiel's cattle and felling his woods. Lochiel, who watched their motions closely, saw the English soldiers come ashore, one-half having hatchets and other tools as a working party, the other half under arms, to protect their operations. Though the difference of numbers was so great, the chieftain vowed that he would make the red soldier (so the English were called from their uniform) pay dear for every bullock or tree which he should destroy on the black soldier's property (alluding to the dark colour of the tartan, and perhaps to his own complexion). He then demanded of some of his followers who had served under Montrose, whether they had ever seen the Great Marquis encounter with such unequal numbers. They answered, they could recollect no instance of such temerity. 'We will fight, nevertheless,' said Evan Dhu; 'and if each of us kill a man, which is no mighty matter, I will answer for the event.' That his family might not be destroyed in so doubtful an enterprise, he ordered his brother Allan to be bound to a tree, meaning to prevent his interference in the conflict. But Allan prevailed on a little boy, who was left to attend him, to unloose the cords, and was soon as deep in the fight as Evan himself.

"The Camerons, concealed by the trees, advanced so close on the enemy as to pour on them an unexpected and destructive shower of shot and arrows, which slew thirty men; and ere they could recover from their surprise, the Highlanders were in the midst of them, laying about them with incredible fury, with their ponderous swords and axes. After a gallant resistance, the mass of the English began to retire towards their vessels, when Evan Dhu commanded a piper and a small party to go betwixt the enemy and their barks, and then sound his pibroch and war-cry, till their clamour made it seem that there was another body of Highlanders in ambush to cut off their retreat. The English, driven to fury and despair by this new alarm, turned back, like brave men, upon the first assailants; and if the working party had possessed military weapons, Lochiel might have had little reason to congratulate himself on the result of this audacious stratagem.

" He himself had a personal rencontre, strongly characteristic of the ferocity of the times. The chief was singled out by an English officer of great personal strength, and as they were separated from the general strife, they fought in single combat for some time. Lochiel was dexterous enough to disarm the Englishman ; but his gigantic adversary suddenly closed on him, and in the struggle which ensued both fell to the ground, the officer uppermost. He was in the act of grasping at his sword, which had fallen near the place where they lay in deadly struggle, and was naturally extending his neck in the same direction, when the Highland chief, making a desperate effort, grasped his enemy by the collar, and snatching with his teeth at the bare and outstretched throat, he seized it as a wild-cat might have done, and kept his hold so fast as so tear out the windpipe. The officer died in this singular manner. Lochiel was so far from disowning or being ashamed of this extraordinary mode of defence, that he was afterwards heard to say it was the sweetest morsel he had ever tasted.

" When Lochiel, thus extricated from the most imminent danger, was able to rejoin his men, he found they had not only pursued the English to the beach, but even into the sea, cutting and stabbing whomever they could overtake."

Sir Walter narrates one or two similar scenes, and proceeds :—

" By such exploits he rendered himself so troublesome, that the English were desirous to have peace with him on any moderate terms. Their overtures were at first rejected, Evan Dhu returning for answer, that he would not abjure the King's authority, even though the alternative was to be his living and dying in the condition of an exile and outlaw. But when it was hinted to him that no express renunciation of the King's authority would be required, and that he was only desired to live in peace under the existing government, the chief made his submission to the existing powers with much solemnity.

" Lochiel came down on this occasion, at the head of his whole clan in arms, to the garrison of Inverlochy. The English forces being drawn up in a line opposite to them, the Camerons laid down their arms in the name of King Charles, and took them up again in that of the States, without any mention of Cromwell, or any disowning of the King's authority. In consequence of this honourable treaty, the last Scotsman who maintained the cause of Charles Stuart submitted to the authority of the republic.

" It is related of this remarkable chieftain, that he slew with his own hand the last wolf that was ever seen in the Highlands of Scotland. Tradition records another anecdote of him. Being benighted, on some party for the battle or the chase, Evan Dhu laid himself down with his followers to sleep in the snow. As he composed himself to rest, he observed that one of his sons, or nephews, had rolled together a great snowball, on which he deposited his head. Indignant at what he considered a mark of effeminacy, he started up and kicked the snowball from under the sleeper's head, exclaiming—'Are you become so luxurious that you cannot sleep without a pillow ?' "

After the accession of James II., Lochiel came to court to obtain pardon for one of his clan, who, being in command of a party of Camerons, had fired by mistake on a body of Athole men, and killed several. He was received with the most honourable distinction, and his request granted. The King desiring to make him a knight, asked the chieftain for his own sword, in order to render the ceremony still more peculiar. Lochiel had ridden up from Scotland—being then the only mode of travelling—and a constant rain had so rusted his trusty broadsword, that at the moment no man could have unsheathed it. Lochiel, affronted at the idea which the courtiers might conceive from his not being able to draw his own sword, burst into tears.

" ' Do not regard it, my faithful friend,' said King James, with ready courtesy ; ' your sword would have left the scabbard of itself, had the Royal cause required it.'

" With that he bestowed the intended honour with his own sword, which he presented to the new knight as soon as the ceremony was performed."

But Sir Evan Cameron was not destined to go down into his grave before he had occasion to draw the King's sword more than once. The Western Highlands were constantly disturbed during the remaining years of the seventeenth century, and Lochiel figures in every event which took place within sight of Ben Nevis. All the clans whose homes were on its slopes took part in the war which followed the accession of William the Third. The Macintoshes and the Macdonalds took the opportunity to renew their ancient feuds respecting the possession of Glen Roy and Glen Spean, which lie close to the mountain on the north. The Macdonalds of Glencoe and those of Glengarry, which lie a little further off, willingly joined in the fray, and came to help their kinsmen of Keppoch. The Macintoshes met this array at Mullroy.

A furious battle ensued, and the Macintoshes were defeated. The Macphersons now appeared on the scene. Cluny, their chief, took the part of the defeated clan; and having compelled the Macdonalds to submit, set the chief of Macintosh, who had been taken prisoner, at liberty again. But the matter was not to end here; for some soldiers of the Government, under the command of a Captain Mackenzie of Suddie, had taken part in the fight, and Suddie had been killed. Sixty dragoons and two hundred foot-guards were sent down from headquarters with orders to waste the country, and Macdonald of Keppoch had to fly for a time; but a fine having been paid for him, he shortly returned, and soon after-wards we find him besieging Inverness to punish the inhabitants for taking part against him in his late troubles. While engaged in this enterprise, he was interrupted by Lord Dundee—who is better known in history as "Claverhouse"—who persuaded him to join the army he had raised for the restoration of King James. Sir Evan Cameron of Lochiel, and many another chief from the same country, were in the army; and when they met King William's forces under Mackay at Killiecrankie, it was old Lochiel who pointed out a favourable omen to his fellows :—

"The armies shouted when they came in sight of each other; but the enthusiasm of Mackay's soldiers being damped by the circumstances we have observed, their military shout made but a dull and sullen sound compared to the yell of the Highlanders, which rung far and shrill from all the hills around them. Sir Evan Cameron of Lochiel, of whom I formerly gave you some anecdotes, called on those around him to attend to this circum-stance, saying, that in all his battles he observed victory had ever been on the side of those whose shout before joining seemed most sprightly and confident."

This was the last battle in which he took part. He was allowed to retire to his estates after the final success of King William, and there he lived to a great age in peace. Latterly, he grew very infirm, and lost his strength and the use of his faculties, else perhaps he might have prevented the temporary ruin of his family when his eldest son, John Cameron, joined the Earl of Mar in the Old Pretender's rising. However, he survived his son's attainder and flight, and at last "this once formidable warrior was fed like an infant, and, like an infant, rocked in a cradle."

But the history of the Camerons of Lochiel is by no means all there is of interest to be told of Ben Nevis. We mentioned above the invasion of Argyllshire by Donald Balloch, in 1431. This was the occasion of the famous "pibroch," or march, "of Donald Dhu," which Sir Walter Scott's spirited lines have rendered so familiar. The words are full of local allusions :—

> " Pibroch of Donuil Dhu—
> Pibroch of Donuil,
> Wake thy wild voice anew
> Summon Clan Connil.
> Come away, come away,
> Hark to the summons !
> Come in your war array,
> Gentles and Commons.

> " Come from deep glen, and
> From mountain so rocky ;
> The war-pipe and pennon
> Are at Inverlochy.

Come every hill plaid, and
True heart that wears one ;
Come every steel blade, and
Strong hand that bears one."

Inverlochy Castle was the scene of many another such gather-
ing. It is said to have been built originally by Edward the First
of England to overawe the Highlands, and the situation ensured it
a conspicuous part in every contest. It was at Inverlochy that
Donald Dhu defeated Mar and Caithness in 1431 ; and more than
two centuries later, the great Marquis of Montrose surprised
Argyll and his Covenanters under the same walls. He had just
withdrawn towards Inverness, in the winter of 1644, in order to
organise some of the clans for the ensuing campaign ; but during
the last days of January, 1645, " he learned that his rival, Argyll,
had returned into the Western Highlands with some Lowland
forces ; that he had called around him his numerous clan, burning
to revenge the wrongs which they had sustained, and was lying
with a strong force near the old castle of Inverlochy, situated at
the western extremity of the chain of lakes through which the
Caledonian Canal is now conducted.

" The news at once altered Montrose's plans.

" He returned upon Argyll by a succession of the most difficult
mountain-passes covered with snow, and the vanguard of the
Campbells saw themselves suddenly engaged with that of their
implacable enemy. Both parties lay all night on their arms ; but,
by break of day, Argyll betook himself to his galley, and rowing
off shore, remained a spectator of the combat, when, by all the rules
of duty and gratitude, he ought to have been at the head of his

devoted followers. His unfortunate clansmen supported the honour of the name with the greatest courage, and many of the most distinguished fell on the field of battle. Montrose gained a complete victory, which greatly extended his influence over the Highlands, and in proportion diminished that of his discomfited rival."

With a purpose very similar to that which had caused Edward the First to build Inverlochy, General Monk built the fort, afterwards strengthened and called after William the Third. Even this fortress is now no longer used for its original purpose. It has passed into private hands, having been sold by Government to Campbell of Monzie. Yet Fort-William was not without its place in history. At least twice it comes forward very prominently. The first time was soon after its construction. In 1692, William the Third having tried in vain to pacify the Highlands, issued a proclamation, in which the last day of the year was named as the latest date at which the submission of the chiefs would be received; and further announcing that those clans who had not by their heads taken the oath of allegiance before the 31st December would be looked upon and treated as public enemies. The humane and wise object of this proclamation was attended with considerable success. After some hesitation, and a show of force on the part of the Government, the chiefs, one after another, came in before the period had elapsed; but there was one exception. Macdonald of Glencoe, as we saw above, was one of the chiefs implicated in the affair at Mullroy. The clan was one of the most turbulent, and the year had almost elapsed without any formal act of submission on the part of MacIan, their representative. On the last day of December, however, Glencoe appeared at Fort-William, and offered to take the oath of allegiance. Colonel Hill, the governor of the fort, was not an officer of sufficient rank, nor a magistrate, to take the oath tendered him, and Macdonald was desired to repair to Inverary, to the Sheriff of Argyleshire, Sir Colin Campbell, to swear allegiance. But Inverary was at that season four or five days' journey from Glencoe, and the first week of a new year had nearly gone by before the faith of the Macdonalds had been pledged. Regarding the subsequent event, which shed such a gloomy light over Glencoe, much controversy has taken place. We are not concerned to vindicate the character of either William or his minister, the Master of Stair. There can be no doubt the Campbells and other neighbouring clans had powerful friends at court, and carried their bloody feuds and barbarous quarrels even into the civilised life of the capital. Sanguinary instructions were sent to Colonel Hill. The tribe of Glencoe was to be extirpated ; they had been named in a proclamation made on the 16th January :—" As for MaeIan of Glencoe and that tribe, if they can be well distinguished from the rest of the Highlanders, it will be proper, for the vindication of public justice, to extirpate that set of thieves "—words, no doubt, very shocking to our ears ; but when we consider the lawless character of the country at the time, they can scarcely be considered too severe. Whether the knowledge of Glencoe's submission was purposely suppressed or not can never be known, in all probability ; but much of our pity for the victims of the error, if it was one, is removed when we remember that both they and most of their neighbours, if not all, had long since, by repeated acts of disorder and even of blood, justly forfeited their lives. A party of soldiers was ordered to occupy Glencoe on the 1st of February, where, being received as friends by the Macdonalds, and accounting for their coming on the plea that Fort-William was overcrowded, they remained for nearly a fortnight. This gave the subsequent event still more the appearance of treachery. On the 12th, orders arrived that all the members of the clan under seventy years of age were to be put to death. Campbell of Glenlyon, who commanded the soldiers, though he was a connection by marriage of the chief, and though he had enjoyed his hospitality on several occasions, does not seem to have had much hesitation in executing these orders.

"About four o'clock, in the morning of 13th February, the scene of blood began. A party, commanded by one of the Lindsays, came to MacIan's house and knocked for admittance, which was at once given. Lindsay, one of the expected guests at the family meal of the day, commanded this party, who instantly shot MacIan dead by his own bed-side, as he was in the act of dressing himself, and giving orders for refreshments to be provided for his fatal visitors. His aged wife was stripped by the savage soldiery, who, at the same time, drew off the gold rings from her fingers with their teeth. She died the next day, distracted with grief, and the brutal treatment she had received. Several domestics and clansmen were killed at the same place.

.   .   .   .

"Meantime the work of death proceeded with as little remorse as Stair himself could have desired. Even the slight mitigation of their orders respecting those above seventy years was disregarded by the soldiery in their indiscriminate thirst for blood, and several

very aged and bedridden persons were slain amongst others. At
the hamlet where Glenlyon had his own quarters, nine men,
including his landlord, were bound and shot like felons;
and one of them, Macdonald of Auchintriaten, had General
Hill's passport in his pocket at the time. A fine lad of twenty
had, by some glimpse of compassion on the part of the soldiers,
been spared, when one Captain Drummond came up, and
demanding why the orders were transgressed in that particular, caused him instantly to be put to death. A boy, five or
six years old, clung to Glenlyon's knees, entreating for mercy,
and offering to become his servant for life, if he would spare
him. Glenlyon was moved; but the same Drummond stabbed
the child with his dirk, while he was in this agony of supplication."
Out of a population of about two hundred, nearly a quarter were
put to death in this cold-blooded manner, and probably many more
perished from cold and hunger. "Flying from their burning huts,
and from their murderous visitors, the half-naked fugitives committed themselves to a winter morning of darkness, snow, and
storm, amidst a wilderness the most savage in the West Highlands,
having a bloody death behind them, and before them tempest,
famine, and desolation. Bewildered in the snow-wreaths, several
sank to rise no more. But the severities of the storm were tender
mercies compared to the cruelty of their persecutors. The great
fall of snow, which proved fatal to several of the fugitives, was the
means of saving the remnant that escaped. Major Duncanson,
agreeably to the plan expressed in his orders to Glenlyon, had not
failed to put himself in motion, with four hundred men, on the
evening preceding the slaughter; and had he reached the eastern

passes out of Glencoe by four in the morning, as he calculated, he must have intercepted and destroyed all those who took that only way of escape from Glenlyon and his followers. But as this reinforcement arrived so late as eleven in the forenoon, they found no Macdonald alive in Glencoe, save an old man of eighty, whom they slew; and, after burning such houses as were yet unconsumed, they collected the property of the tribe, consisting of twelve hundred head of cattle and horses, besides goats and sheep, and drove them off to the garrison of Fort-William."

Fort-William once more appears in history. It was besieged in 1746 by the Young Pretender, but without success. It is worth noting that, notwithstanding the massacre, Macdonald of Glencoe joined his standard with a hundred and fifty men, and, according to Scott, had an opportunity, during the march into the Lowlands, of sparing the house of the Earl of Stair, to whose father the clan owed so great an injury.

We have several times had occasion to speak of Glen Roy. Modern science has given it an interest even greater than any it had as the scene of the last great battle of the clans. Mr. Geikie thus describes the " Parallel Roads" of Glen Roy :—

" Far away up the valley, if the day be a favourable one, the traveller can trace a line carved along the steep hill-side, to the south of the river, and running with seemingly mathematical precision in a horizontal course till it is lost in the distance. . . . Returning now to Glen Roy, the traveller should ascend that valley to see what light its famous ' Parallel Roads' have to cast upon the history of the old glaciers of the Highlands. The same long, straight line, which, as he drew near to the Bridge of

Roy, he noticed running high along the mountain-side, in the south of the Spean Valley, is now seen to turn up Glen Roy, winding along the hills of that valley with the same singular horizontality. When he gets several miles up the glen, he begins to see traces of two other terraces, until, on reaching a turn of the road, the long, deep glen lies before him, with its three bars, straight and distinct as if they had been drawn with a ruler, yet winding into all the recesses of the steep slopes, and coming out again over the projecting parts without ever deviating from their parallelism. The 'roads,' so long a subject of wonderment and legendary story among the Highlanders, and for so many years a source of sore perplexity among men of science, seem at last to be understood. Each of them is a shelf or terrace, cut by the shore waters of a lake that once filled Glen Roy. The highest is of course the oldest, and those beneath it were formed in succession, as the waters of the lake were lowered. They are seen not only in Glen Roy. A little beyond where the first good view of the lake is obtained, there is a hollow through the hills on the left side of the valley, marked on the maps as gap. This hollow forms a short 'col' between Glen Roy and a small valley that strikes away to the south-west. Standing on the top of the ridge, the observer looks up Glen Roy on the one side, and down this narrow valley on the other, and he can mark that, while the lowest of the parallel roads in Glen Roy runs along the hill-side, a short way below him the two upper roads come through the hollow, and wind westward into Glen Collarig ; so that the old lake not only filled up Glen Roy, but also some of the other valleys to the west. Until Agassiz suggested the idea of a dam of glacier-ice, the great difficulty in the way of understanding how a lake could ever have filled these valleys, was the entire absence of any relic of the barrier that must have kept back the water. Mr. Jamieson has recently shown, however, that Agassiz's suggestion is fully borne out by the evidence of great glacial erosion, both in Glen Spean, and in the valley of the Caledonian Canal. The latter valley, as I have already pointed out, seems to have been filled to the brim with ice, which, choking up the mouth of Glen Gluoy and Glen Spean, served to pond back the waters of these glens. The Glen Ireig glacier, in like manner, stretched right across Glen Spean, and mounted its north bank. When the lake that must thus have filled Glen Roy and the neighbouring valleys was at its deepest, its surplus waters would escape from the head of Glen Roy down into Strath Spey, and at that time the uppermost beach or parallel road (1140 feet above the present sea-level) was formed. The Glen Ireig glacier then shrank a little, and the lake was thus lowered about eighty feet, so as to form the middle terrace, which is 1059 feet above the sea, the outflow being now by the head of Glen Glaster, and through Loch Laggan into the Spey. After the lake had remained for a time at that height, the Glen Ireig glacier continued on the decline, and at last crept back out of Glen Spean. By this means the level of the lake was reduced to 847 feet above the sea, and the waters of Glen Roy joined those of Loch Laggan, forming the long winding lake, having its overflow by what is now the head of Glen Spean, into Strath Spey. While this level was maintained, the lowest of the parallel roads of Glen Roy was formed. As the climate of the glacial period grew milder, however, the mass of ice which choked up the mouth of Glen Spean, and ponded back the water, gradually melted away. The drainage of Glen Roy, Glen Spean, and their tributary valleys was then no longer arrested, and as the lake crept step by step down the glen towards the sea, the streams one by one took their places in the channels, which they have been busy widening and deepening ever since. Such seems to have been the history of the mysterious parallel roads of Lochaber. Instead of tracing back their origin to the days of Fingal, they stand before us as the memorials of an infinitely vaster antiquity—the shores, as it were, of a phantom lake, that came into being with the growth of the glaciers, and vanished as they melted away."

Marcus Ward & Co., Printers, Royal Ulster Works, Belfast.

CPSIA information can be obtained
at www.ICGtesting.com
Printed in the USA
BVHW080422231118
533756BV00029B/1072/P